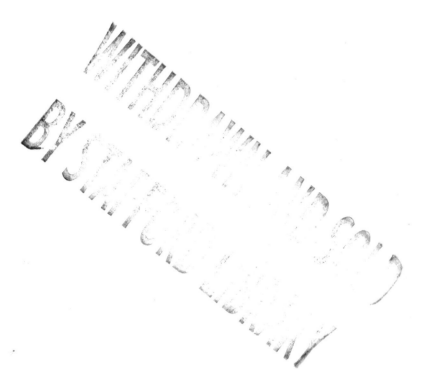

DEFEAT OF THE WOLF PACKS

DEFEAT OF THE WOLF PACKS

Geoffrey P. Jones

WILLIAM KIMBER · LONDON

First published in 1986 by
WILLIAM KIMBER & CO. LIMITED
100 Jermyn Street, London, SW1Y 6EE

© Geoffrey P. Jones, 1986

ISBN 0–7183–0589–2/502

*Typeset by Grove Graphics, Tring
and printed in Great Britain by
Redwood Burn, Trowbridge, Wiltshire*

Contents

List of Illustrations

Acknowledgements

After my research for this book, I was still left with many questions that needed answering; the following people were good enough to respond:

The editor of *Navy News*, and through his columns, W. J. Adeldel (Wells), G. J. Auld (Tayport), F. C. A. Ball (Reading), P. Bird (Queensland), J. Cannon (Essex), L. Cheeseman (Weymouth) D. J. Collingwood (Wantage), J. Creasey (Kettering) H. N. Davies (Accrington) R. Feasey (Bournemouth), C. S. Gould (Gillingham), C. Green (Littlehampton), G. Haddon (South Africa) J. W. Kennedy (Dulwich), S. Lawrence (Cosham), W. Laycock (Blackburn), R. Loader (London), W. McEvoy (Moreton), R. Mendoza (Westcliffe), C. Osborne (Ipswich), N. R. Pashe (Heston) and R. S. C. Robinson (Portsmouth).

Specific U-boat help was obtained from R. M. Coppock (*U-377* and *U-972*), J. O. Krieg (*U-81*), Jak Mallmann Showell (*U-377*), H. D. Speidel (*U-81*) and G. Kelbling (*U-593*) answered via Gordon Haddon.

Former U-boat crew members who also helped were H. Guske (*U-764*), J. Hellmanns (*U-643*), and K. Wahnig (*U-802*)

Research facilities were made available to me at the Imperial War Museum and Public Record Office. I visited the Royal Navy Submarine Museum at Gosport where Richard Compton-Hall and Gus Britton were most helpful, and the MOD (Navy) answered some questions.

In America the Grumman Aircraft Corporation of New York and the US Navy Department in Washington gave excellent co-operation.

My brother Ted, in Australia, contributed the diagram.

To all these kind people who helped, or offered to help, I am sincerely grateful and at the same time I will absolve them from any mistakes, which must be mine.

Copyright photographs were provided by: Australian War Memorial, Jim Creasey, D. K. Gowland, Grumman Aircraft Corp, Gordon Haddon, Imperial War Museum, John W. Kennedy, Bill Laycock, Jak Mallmann Showell, N. R. Pashe, A. & J. Pavia, Dave Sexby and the US Navy Dept.

GPJ
Abbey Wood
1986

Introduction

This book is about U-boats, their crews and the hunters that sank them in the mid-winter of 1943/44. During this time there occurred the breaking up of the wolf packs, U-boats operating in groups.

As the season commences the wolf packs, with their acoustic torpedoes, are still a force to be reckoned with, but gradually they are broken up into smaller groups. No one can put an exact date on when the wolf packs were defeated; it could even be argued that their potential still constituted a threat until the last day of the war. However, during the period covered in the text, some of the U-boats lost had carried out many successful attacks on well known naval ships as well as merchant vessels. The plans for the U-boats' destruction and the execution of such plans are studied as indeed are the stories of the ones that got away.

It is impossible to write such a book in strict chronological sequence, although I have tried to do this wherever possible. When the subject covers accidental losses and losses from bombing raids, combined sea and air attacks, destruction from sea-based and land-based aircraft and striking mines as well as losses from United States Navy and Army aircraft, American, British and Canadian warships and RAF aircraft, this is just not practicable. I have written my chapters in such a way that I hope the narrative will keep the reader's attention until the chapter ends and he is thus not distracted by an odd incident that should be chronologically inserted.

It is now well established that at this period of the war the British were reading most of the U-boat signals and attempting to act accordingly. The Germans had to rely on what information they could glean by U-boat sightings, aircraft reconnaissance and reading of other than naval signals as they had singularly failed to

11

cryptoanalyse Royal Navy codes, which had been changed in mid-1943.

By the time the book ends at the end of January 1944 Admiral Dönitz had realised that the Battle of the Atlantic, using conventional U-boats in packs, could not continue without heavy losses and he was proved right in mid-February when the last centrally directed wolf pack operation in that area ended with heavy losses for the Kriegsmarine.

I have attempted to keep the book balanced by recording the achievements of U-boat crews as well as the forces that hunted them. All were brave men who served their respective countries with distinction.

CHAPTER ONE

The First Four Years

Intelligence reports at the start of the war indicated that Germany had 49 operational U-boats, with immediate plans for the building of many more. From the outbreak, attacks on merchant shipping were severe but they by no means reached disastrous proportions. Nevertheless, the loss of 154,000 tons in the first month gave ample indication of the struggle ahead.

The convoy system, which was so successful during the Kaiser's war, was immediately instituted. Initially station-keeping was poor; signals and W/T procedures required polishing and reorganizing but, all in all, the system was quite successful, well indicated by the fact that during October 2,301 ships were escorted and only seven of these were torpedoed.

By the end of the month there were 149 destroyers, 8 patrol vessels, 33 escort vessels and 107 trawlers engaged in anti-U-boat activities, all based at strategic points at home and abroad.

German tactics were not well developed and their major effort was spent in sinking unescorted ships and in sowing magnetic mines in the vicinity of British ports. Some convoys were attacked but in general the U-boats were very reluctant to expose themselves to depth charge attack, preferring instead to nip off stragglers and independent neutrals.

One clear indication of future German tactics was the marked preference of some U-boat commanders for night attacks on the surface, retiring at high speed; indeed in the U-boat commanders' handbook the instructions for movements were clearly set out:

After a night attack surfaced the commander must do his best to remain surfaced, to observe the results of the attack so as to be later in a favourable position to carry out a second or a third. Do not go deep unless it is necessary. Going deep makes the U-boat blind and feeble. On the surface the commander preserves his freedom of vision, and of action. He must dive therefore, solely and exclusively when an imminent hunt forces him to do so. If, on account of a hunt it is necessary to submerge, begin by going to depth at high speed and move off from the spot at which you fired and from the track of the torpedo. It is useless to worry about the enemy's hydrophones. At night, after a hit, there is such confusion on the surface that the enemy's hydrophone operator cannot hear or locate with certainty any U-boat proceeding submerged. The distance to which it must withdraw submerged depends on visibility. When resurfacing, the enemy should still be in sight, but the U-boat must not be sighted while resurfacing. Usually a withdrawal run of 2,000 to 3,000 metres will be enough.

This night hit-and-run exposed one of the weaknesses of the convoy system.

British anti-U-boat strategy at this time consisted of providing light escorts for convoys, striking forces based at strategic points and in fixed harbour defences. Coastal Command had initiated aircraft patrols and although many sightings were reported, sinkings were almost negligible, mostly because no adequate airborne depth charges had been provided. Meanwhile a building programme was put underway calling for 67 escort destroyers, 92 corvettes and sloops and 43 trawlers.

Throughout January and February 1940, U-boat activity was confined to the fairly well established policy of attacking unescorted shipping and in sowing mines. In mid-January *U-44* sank a Greek ship and later attacked a French convoy off the Portuguese coast. When the convoy was reported Admiral Dönitz, head of the U-boat arm, ordered two further U-boats to the scene. This was the first instance of the wolf pack tactic that had been practised in war games in the thirties. In the event the boats did not attack together.

The policy of unrestricted U-boat warfare, although practised, was definitely adopted by declaration on 18 February. In an obvious attempt to prove to neutrals that it was suicidal to trade with Britain, activity increased in the last two weeks of the month when 160,000 tons were lost.

The first six months of the war were spent by both sides in feeling out the other's strength and in laying plans for future offensive and defensive operations.

In March the U-boat command withdrew all its boats from the areas around the British Isles, except for two or three that had limited success in the period of the full moon; the reason for this retirement was to ensure their readiness to take part in the forthcoming invasion of Norway, which was undertaken in April.

Early in the month every available U-boat had assumed its patrol position for the imminent military operations against Norway. In spite of the fact that every destroyer of the Home Fleet plus many more trawlers were in this area, sinkings by and attacks on U-boats were surprisingly low.

A month after the invasion of Norway saw the blitzkrieg through the Low Countries and France. The tactical situation at sea, however, did not change until June, when large numbers of U-boats came out to operate in the Western Approaches. Sinkings were numerous and were increased by the inglorious entry of the Italians into the fracas.

The strength of the anti-U-boat forces was gently reduced by the evacuation of the troops from France. Of the many taking part, it was inevitable that a considerable number would be sunk, thereby seriously affecting future anti-U-boat operations. In spite of this, only eight ships were sunk in convoy during the period. U-boats took a more active part in the invasion of France; they were particularly active in the Bay of Biscay area where numerous unescorted neutrals were sunk.

The fall of France was a grave blow to the defence of Allied shipping. Germany now had complete control of the European coastline from northern Norway to the Spanish boundary. Although it was some time before the ports obtained could be used for U-boat bases, the month of June marked the opening of a new and intensified period of U-boat activity against the trade routes.

The offensive in the Western Approaches that began early in June continued throughout the summer. It was natural that, exuberant with the successes of their land armies, the attacks should be pressed home with increased vigour. The north-west Atlantic convoy route was definitely established during the month; ships assembling in

Halifax, Nova Scotia and sailing together, were to be met outside the U-boat danger area by local forces and escorted as far as possible. The only protection afforded these convoys in mid-ocean was the presence of Armed Merchant Cruisers and occasional heavier forces.

The menace to shipping increased with the newly constructed U-boats that were being completed and rushed into operation. The first indication of pack tactics appeared in July when a convoy from Canada was attacked with the loss of six ships. Despite this the convoy system continued to be successful.

In the handbook issued to U-boat commanders the following instructions were given:

. . . in the case of a U-boat ordered to keep contact, attacks must be ordered by the Operational Control. For the information of other U-boats transmit your own decision to attack by means of short signal, according to the *Handbook of Short Signals*. The possible disadvantage of putting the enemy on his guard by this wireless transmission is always less important than the other, namely, that for lack of information the other U-boats cannot come up with the target.

Besides reports relating to your own attack, reports of contact should be given regularly and accurately, in the order given in the following instructions:

(a) The first two U-boats in contact, acting as actual shadowers, must give full reports every hour.

(b) Until the first two U-boats give the above-described contact reports, the others, as soon as they are near, must transmit once only the short signal 'Have lost contact'.

(c) If a shadower has not reported for over an hour-and-a-half, another U-boat must immediately take over, without waiting for an order to do so.

(d) If a shadower loses contact it must report as soon as possible the last position, course and speed of the enemy.

(e) The other U-boats which have been in contact and have fallen astern from being submerged for a long time, or on account of an anti-U-boat hunt, must report their own position as well.

Even shadowing U-boats must operate as best suits their own attack. They must not prejudice their own manoeuvre to reach the sectors ahead, thus jeopardizing their own attack, by approaching too near the enemy in order to get better data. Transmissions of D/F signals by the shadower make it much easier for the other U-boats to approach the enemy. They must be made at the request of the other U-boats or by order of the High Command ashore, or, in certain circumstances, on its own initiative if no such order has been received in time and it has reason to consider it useful, every half-hour on a fixed long wave in the usual way through bearing and D/F signals. If the commander decides to transmit D/F signals of his own accord, the other U-boats must first be warned of this by W/T message.

For keeping contact and for approach manoeuvre the following rules apply:

(a)   Carry out the manoeuvre of improving the inclination at the extreme limits of visibility. Remain absolutely unobserved.

(b)   Keep contact by observing the tops of the masts or the smoke. Smoke is quite sufficient. If it disappears temporarily, this does not mean that you have lost contact. Only if nothing shows for some time need you close to regain contact.

(c)   Keep a very careful look-out, report at once if the tops of the masts appear and begin to lengthen, and move off at full speed. At the same time contrive not to lose distance but proceed ahead. If you are still close, submerge and go to periscope depth. Surface again as soon as the situation clears up.

(d)   If your own position is astern of the convoy, do not let yourself be forced too far to the rear by manoeuvres of the rear escort, but submerge in time. This saves a great deal of distance and a lot of time in overtaking again.

(e)   Keep a very careful look-out on the opposite side to the enemy as well. It is easy to be surprised on this side by ships of the convoy coming from the van and proceeding towards the sides or the rear, or by escort ships, serving as remote escort, approaching the convoy.

In addition to the cautious, tactical procedure of the shadowing U-boat which is pressing towards the van, it is of decisive importance for the operation of the other U-boats that they should all steer faultlessly, especially the one which made the contact. In the operational area therefore, it is the imperative duty of the Commander to navigate always most accurately, availing himself of all possible means. For this purpose it is necessary by day to estimate the boat's position several times if possible. Cultivate this habit to acquire the sense of loss of speed and of drift. If errors of position are found, the shadower's reports must be corrected at once with reference to the error and, as required, by all the other U-boats which discover errors of position in the reports of the shadower.

In August an exchange was made with the United States whereby the British received fifty last war American destroyers. Some of these were turned over to Canada; all were rushed into operation as soon as anti-U-boat installations were fitted. These ships were old and required much attention, but they filled a gap and their presence did much to bolster morale. September and October saw night attacks pressed home more savagely than ever, and with considerable success. Because of the grave danger of invasion, a large part of the light forces were drawn to the east coast with the inevitable reaction in favour of the U-boats.

The establishment of air bases in the area of the Western Approaches enabled Coastal Command to provide more and more air coverage for convoys, and U-boats became increasingly wary of surfacing in the vicinity of Britain. Extending the minefields to the westward also helped to persuade the U-boats to keep further from shore, forcing them well out into the open Atlantic. Attacks generally developed after a convoy had been spotted and shadowed until dark, when it was attacked. The U-boat would then position itself ahead of the convoy for another attack.

Pack attacks were also formed up by long range reconnaissance aircraft that signalled to U-boat control the position, course and speed of the sighted convoys. This was quite successful until counter measures in the form of CAM ships and shore-based aircraft proved too much for the Luftwaffe.

The small pack attacks that had taken place were sure indications of future German tactics and showed up weaknesses, which soon led to the birth of many new counter-measures. At this time, however, all that could be done was to dispose the escort screens to give the maximum protection. The necessity of finding some means of detecting U-boats on the surface was recognised and the highest priority was given to the development of this device. The final result was the almost magical appearance of radar, though it was not to be in general use for several months to come.

In November it was apparent that U-boat tactics had fallen into a definite pattern; suitable countermeasures were employed and sinkings were appreciably less. Day attacks by U-boats were abandoned as policy but were delivered where opportunity presented itself. Night attacks were generally delivered from the beam of the convoy. U-boats cut in astern of the bow escorts and pressed home some attacks from close range.

Convoy escort tactics were only fairly successful and consisted of sweeping out likely or suspected areas, illuminating with starshell, and engaging the U-boats whenever possible. Two very important aids were still lacking, radar and R/T. The latter was fitted just as quickly as production facilities would allow and this proved of great assistance as it provided a means whereby escort groups could easily be controlled to take combined offensive action.

It was realised by escort commanders that if a U-boat could be detected on the surface, it could be forced to dive by gunfire and then depth-charged until destroyed or proved no longer to be a menace to the convoy. Every effort was made to accomplish this but unfortunately, the first indication of the presence of a U-boat was usually the torpedoing of one of the ships in convoy.

The lull in U-boat activity, first noticed in November, continued into December. This was partially due to the bombing of their bases by the RAF, particularly Lorient. To aggravate the many other problems, extremely bad weather was encountered during the winter. Its effects caused half the escort forces to be laid up because of damage sustained in violent storms.

The diversion of convoy routes proved to be a most satisfactory method of dodging the enemy. There were not more than thirty U-boats at sea and hence it was physically impossible for them to spot, or if they did, effectively to attack every convoy that sailed. This led, inevitably, to forcing the U-boats farther and farther out to sea in the hopes of intercepting the shipping as soon as possible. Royal Air Force activity also hampered their activities and this, together with the desire for more room to employ their increasing number of U-boats, led to a complete change in the strategical situation.

In March, an air base was established in Iceland for the protection of northerly routed convoys. It was felt necessary to extend the area of escort operations, and while the local escorts continued to sail out and shepherd the flock through the danger areas, a base was established at Hjalfiord.

Radar was proving to have limitations due to the many back echoes, but this was remedied to a large extent and in March *U-100*, the first U-boat to be detected by this device, was sunk.

Early in April a Canadian-UK convoy was viciously attacked with the attendant loss of ten ships, and in May another was attacked before the local escort forces had joined. The time had come to extend the field of escort operations and a base was at once established at St John's Newfoundland. The Royal Canadian Navy took most of this new burden and all Canadian destroyers and corvettes were immediately sent there for duty.

In June, 25 of the 35 U-boats at sea were operating in the North Atlantic. Convoy HX133 was attacked and in spite of great efforts by the U-boats only five ships were sunk, for the loss of two attackers. Sightings reported off Cape Race and Greenland indicated the pains that the Germans were taking to try to locate the convoys. As the convoys were being escorted from Newfoundland, activities were naturally extended to provide protection from Halifax; this was initiated in July.

During the month the U-boats seemed to withdraw to the eastwards, possibly to avoid contact with American patrol vessels. New methods of attack were under development, notably the one ton Mark X depth charge, and the hedgehog, a new ahead throwing weapon.

August was quiet, although for the first time an escort vessel was attacked, an indication of future policy. In September several attacks were pressed home on convoys with severe losses. No new tactics were employed by the Germans, with the exception that they operated in larger packs. Twelve U-boats operated against SC42 and sank fifteen ships.

Heavy attacks were also delivered against the next three convoys.

These were costly but the strong offensive action of escort forces indicated that they were slowly seizing the initiative from the U-boat commanders. Owing to the destruction of many of the U-boats and their crews, the new boats were mostly manned by inexperienced crews. Auxiliary aircraft carriers made their first appearance, and to good effect. Meanwhile air coverage from shore increased both in hours and in technique.

November was a good month for the Atlantic forces; evasive routing offered great obstacles to the U-boats, but at the same time could not be relied upon for sole protection in view of the large numbers of U-boats at sea.

On 7 December the Pearl Harbor attack by the Japanese brought the United States openly into the now world-wide conflict. Their entry changed the entire strategic situation in the Atlantic and German control lost no time in exploiting it. Towards the end of the month there was an appreciable movement of U-boats to the westward, signifying the beginning of many melancholy months for the Allies.

Owing to the special American commitments in the Far East, Britain and Canada assumed the responsibility of carrying almost all the anti-U-boat warfare in the Atlantic. Since there were simply not enough ships adequately to protect the total eastern seaboard of North America, U-boat commanders were free to choose their victims at will, and did!

Over 80 U-boats were operational and by far the largest proportion were stationed along the American coast at such focal points as Cape Hatteras, New York and Boston. They kept well clear of escorted convoys and generally played havoc with independently sailed ships; of 270,000 tons sunk in January 1942 only 12,000 were lost while in convoy.

The situation that developed in January continued throughout the entire year. Most of the German effort was spent in sinking tankers and when their activity was extended to the Caribbean area, very severe losses followed. The numbers of U-boats continued to increase and it was not until the summer, when the escort situation permitted the introduction of the convoy system, that the outlook improved.

By July, radar was in general use and proved to be a remarkable success. The U-boat had been robbed of its night security and it was no longer possible for packs to attack undetected. H/F D/F facilities had been extended to many ships and this further enabled senior officers to take adequate evasive and offensive action.

The hedgehog was being fitted in escort vessels as rapidly as possible, though no indication of its success was immediately forthcoming. The Mark X depth charge proved to be of good value under the special conditions for which it was designed. The power of these charges was so great that it was necessary to reassure some of the escort commanders of their safety in using them.

A large number of U-boats were operating in the vicinity of northern Norway, along supply routes to Russia. The combined operations of U-boats, aircraft, surface ships and four weather boats made the trip to Murmansk a most unpleasant one for everyone concerned.

As was expected, as soon as the Germans met any organized opposition in the West Indies area, they promptly looked for a new soft spot, which they found off South Africa. In October 1942 a group of a dozen boats was operating off the Capetown and Indian Ocean regions at any one time.

At this time the *Pillenwerfer*, or submarine bubble target, was reported used by the Germans. This was a device that ejected chemical pills which activated on contact with sea water and created a disturbance which effected a false asdic contact. Initially asdic operators on escorts could not distinguish between the disturbance and the target, so frequently the U-boat escaped.

Severe shipping losses were sustained in the Atlantic in October and November due to the increased numbers of U-boats operating along the convoy trade routes, while sinkings in the Caribbean were still high. A large number of escorts were detailed to assist in the invasion of North Africa and this further reacted to the detriment of the Atlantic escort forces. November 1942 saw the highest shipping losses of the war, some 705,000 tons in one month.

Losses dropped sharply in December and January; the U-boats made an effort to hamper the North African operations but were completely frustrated by escorts and land based aircraft. Yet sinkings were still high, on the wrong side of half-a-million tons each month.

January 1943 saw the combined Chiefs of Staff meeting at

Casablanca and they laid down that in the coming year the defeat of the U-boat should be the first charge on their combined resources. In Germany Karl Dönitz took command of the whole Kriegsmarine with the rank of Grossadmiral, but he still kept in very close touch with U-boat headquarters. Losses in the month gave a completely false impression of the extremely serious tactical situation to be faced by Allied forces. The fate of one convoy, bound for Gibraltar from Trinidad, gave a somewhat truer picture, when seven of nine tankers were torpedoed and sunk.

Evasive routings continued to be successful but had ceased to be relied upon as an effective protective measure. With the numbers of U-boats as large as it was, it became more and more difficult to route convoys through relatively safe areas. It was increasingly evident that the tempo was stepping up, and that the critical phase of the Battle of the Atlantic could not be far in the future.

Never had U-boat headquarters so concentrated their forces for just one objective as they did in February, with the avowed purpose of severing Britain's lifeline. Two convoys were heavily attacked and while losses were not light, the spirited offensive action of the escorts resulted in the destruction of several U-boats.

The onslaught continued into March. Evasive routing and bad weather hampered the Germans, but as long as they had wolf-packs at sea, evasive tactics certainly could not be relied upon especially as the Germans at this time were reading Admiralty signals and were able to position their boats across a convoy's path. Sinkings increased as 630,000 tons were lost in seven convoys.

With April, the offensive waned. U-boats failed to press home an attack when favourably disposed to do so. Attacks were delivered, some even vigorously but U-boats made a poor showing. The combined weight of escort forces, support and air support groups, long range aircraft and new weapons; together with professional skill gained through hard training, proved almost too much for the Germans. The use of auxiliary aircraft carriers, thrown into the battle at the last minute, had provided much needed air coverage and enabled convoys to be sailed on the easier though longer southern route.

U-boat headquarters accepted defeat in the spring battle of the Atlantic and most U-boats were withdrawn from the trade routes;

41 boats had been lost in all theatres of operations during May and this rate of attrition could not be allowed to continue. Considerable effort was spent in June trying to overcome the convoys to Casablanca but successes were very limited. Although U-boats had been withdrawn from the Atlantic a few were dispersed along the eastern seaboard of the United States, with indifferent results.

Now the British seized the initiative and began the Bay of Biscay offensive. Practically every U-boat at sea had to pass through the Bay en route to and from its patrol position, and here was to be the next great theatre of operations.

A large number of escort vessels were sent to the Bay and with the full cooperation of the RAF successes were both high and gratifying. Increased efficiency was displayed by the escorts and if a U-boat was detected by two or three vessels, its destruction was pretty well assured. The Second Support Group, commanded by Captain F. J. Walker, earned an enviable record during these happy days. One of the effects of this campaign was immediately apparent. Owing to the loss of several supply U-boats, the boats that were operating in the West Indies were forced to return to their bases a fortnight earlier than usual, thereby limiting their capabilities and easing the situation in that theatre.

From the beginning of July the Germans were unable to break the new Royal Navy cyphers, but in the autumn the British U-boat tracking service were reading U-boat signals at much the same time as the U-boat commanders!

Initially hedgehog had not proved as satisfactory as was expected, partially due to the reluctance of commanding officers to use it; as there was no explosion except on contact, there was no morale value to the weapon either detrimental to the U-boat crews or bolstering to the escorts' crews.

As anticipated, operations against the North Atlantic trade routes recommenced in September and a large part of the escort forces operating in the Bay were sent back to convoy duty. The introduction of a new weapon in the form of an acoustic homing torpedo gave two convoys and their escorts a gruelling four days; though three escorts were lost, the U-boat pack was badly mauled.

Successes for the Allies continued into October when 26 U-boats were sunk, mostly in the North Atlantic. To counter aircraft attacks,

Running in to Brest. With a damaged hull *U-377* follows its escort

U-boats were now being fitted, or re-fitted, with quadruple oerlikons and either one 37mm automatic cannon or two singly mounted oerlikons on a widened bandstand.

On 12 October a ripple of polite laughter greeted the announcement made by Winston Churchill in the House of Commons that by virtue of an alliance concluded by Portugal and Britain in 1373 the Portuguese government, at the request of HM Government had granted to the Allies the use of the Azores. The occupation of these strategically placed islands, where sea escorts could put into the bays to refuel and where aircraft could be based, was soon put to good use. On 9 November *U-707* was the first victim of an Azores-based aircraft. This occupation, and other factors during the next three months, shortly to be examined in detail, marked the beginning of a campaign which was to defeat the wolf packs.

CHAPTER TWO

Beginning of the Winter

October 1943 had been a bad month for U-boat Command; 26 boats were destroyed. Five more U-boats were lost in the first nine days of November. For the second time in the year, following the destruction of 41 U-boats in May, the scale of losses, not matched with compensating successes, was becoming unacceptable.

All the Type XIV U-tankers had been sunk and the Atlantic U-boats had necessarily to spend less time on patrol as they were not being refuelled at sea. The staff at headquarters decided the most practical solution, in the circumstances, was to move groups of U-boats southwards, to the Gibraltar area, in an attempt to intercept convoys passing nearer their Biscay bases. Boats were also ordered to proceed submerged by day and only surface at night.

Unfortunately for the Germans, the occupation of the Azores in October meant that Coastal Command could make three-pronged attacks on the new dispositions. Aircraft from the United Kingdom, from Gibraltar and the Azores could provide almost continuous air escort to supplement the increasing numbers of sea escorts that were becoming available to protect the convoys.

Strangely then, the first U-boat attacked in this period was accounted for by English-based aircraft. The high numbered U-boat, *U-966*, was launched just ten months earlier, in the middle of January 1943, from the Blohm and Voss yard in Hamburg, a Type VIIC boat. Oberleutnant Ekkehard Wolf was its first, and only, commander. The initial cruise was a four-day one from Kiel to Bergen on 9 September. The U-boat moved on to Trondheim and it was from this Norwegian base that it set out on its first war cruise on 5 October, destination North Atlantic. At the end of the patrol *U-966* was due to put in to a French port and from its position, when attacked, it would appear this is where it was heading when seen by the crew of a Chivenor-based Leigh light Wellington.

26

There was a distinct winter's nip in the air as the aircraft, B-Baker, took off from St Eval at a minute past midnight on 10 November and headed out over the Channel, to the Bay of Biscay area. After four hours in the air the pilot, Warrant Officer L. D. Gunn, was told there was a radar contact at six miles. The Wellington closed and almost immediately the U-boat was clearly seen in the moonlight proceeding on the surface at an estimated ten knots. As the night was clear there was a good chance that the aircraft had not been seen so the Leigh light was not switched on. The Wellington carried out a depth charge attack and two to three minutes later *U-966* dived. The aircraft remained in the area until 0630 when it left for base, touching down safely four hours later.

By this time three Liberators, two USN and one RAF, were airborne and had been directed to the spot by a message from Control. The first E-Easy of the Dunkeswell-based USN 103 Squadron contacted the U-boat by radar after evading two Ju88s. The pilot intended to attack from ahead, but the U-boat altered course at the last moment and the attack developed from the starboard beam. The Mark XV bomb sight was used and five depth charges spaced at 40 feet were released from ninety feet. One depth charge hung up. The rear gunner saw one depth charge enter the water on the port side but did not see the points of entry of the others. The explosions engulfed *U-966* which slowly emerged from the spray and continued on the surface. The Liberator then made a second run and dropped one 600lb depth charge. The U-boat was down by the stern and leaked oil freely. After about half-an-hour *U-966* recovered trim and the oil slick lessened. During both attacks the Germans put up considerable flak from its quadruple cannon. The aircraft returned the fire whenever the range was less than a thousand yards and at least one dead German was seen hanging over the side of the conning tower. The U-boat's fire was not effective and at 1310 the Liberator returned to base.

Another USN Liberator, also E-Easy but of 110 Squadron and also based at Dunkeswell, was next on the scene and found *U-966*, after a radar contact at twenty miles. The U-boat was very low in the water and seas were breaking over the conning tower. The aircraft circled its target and then attacked its starboard bow in the face of light flak. Six depth charges were dropped, which fell

USN Liberator crossing the English coast

correctly for range but 100 feet out for line. The U-boat appeared to roll heavily and turned sharply to port, subsequently zigzagging violently in the general direction of the Spanish coast about fifteen miles away.

At this moment D-Dog of No 311 Squadron arrived. This Czech squadron had been formed in Great Britain at the beginning of August 1940 and had been operating with Liberators since 21 August 1943, out of Chivenor. The 19 Group Liberator, piloted by Flight Sergeant O. Zanda, had taken off at 0810 and as it arrived on the scene *U-966* fired a pyrotechnic which left a double trail of

U-966 under Liberator attack

light blue smoke in the air. The Czech pilot crossed ahead of *U-966*, being unable to make an immediate attack owing to the nearness of high land on the Spanish coast, and then attacked with RP from starboard. One of the first pair of rockets and both of the second pair failed, and the last salvo of four entered the water about fifty feet short of the U-boat, near the bows. None of these was seen to emerge. The U-boat fired at the Liberator without success. After the attack, *U-966* slowed to 6–8 knots and when closing the shore reduced to two knots. When last seen, ninety minutes after the attack, the U-boat was proceeding slowly very close inshore. The first American's attack had damaged *U-966*'s steering; the others inflicted varying damage.

When two hundred yards from the coast a dinghy with eleven of the U-boat's crew made for land. The U-boat beached itself and was blown up by the crew. Eventually 42 of the crew landed at Vivero, twenty miles north of Cape Ortegal, Northern Spain.

On 13 November Air Marshal Sir John Slessor, Commander-in-Chief of Coastal Command, sent a message from his headquarters to 311 Squadron:

> It rather looks as though it must have been your RP attack that sank the U-boat on the coast of Spain on Wednesday – though by the photographs it seems still to have been going strong after the attack. Anyway it's sunk all right, which is the main thing.

The first American attacker was awarded 40 percent of the sinking, the second American ten percent and the Czech aircraft 50 percent – the poor Wellington pilot was not given any credit!

The next boat lost in November was again a victim of a Dunkeswell-based Liberator of the US Navy's VB-103 Squadron under Coastal Command control. This U-boat, *U-508*, commanded by Knight's Cross holder Kapitänleutnant Georg Staats, had been launched from the Hamburg yard of the Deutsche Werke at the end of July 1942. This larger Type IXC$_{40}$ boat carried 22 torpedoes and had a range of 16,800 miles. In a life of under seventeen months *U-508* was to sink fourteen ships with a combined total of 73,692 tons.

After the necessary trials had been successfully carried out *U-508* started its first war cruise, from Kiel-Wik to the Caribbean, on 25 June 1942. It would be the last time that its commander would con any boat from a German port. On, up through the German-garrisoned Danish islands, into the Kattegat, past the Skaw and into the Skagerrak before hitting the real open sea of the North Atlantic.

On this first patrol two small Cuban boats, *Santiago de Cuba* and *Manzanillo* were torpedoed and sunk on 12 August and two others were missed six days later. After nearly three months at sea the patrol ended at Lorient on 17 September.

The second war cruise, from the French base, started exactly one month later. It was to the area around Trinidad, where the tankers loaded, and the crew realised that they would probably not be home in time to celebrate Christmas and the New Year. They did, however, have plenty of successes to celebrate. On 7 November the American 7,176 ton ship *Nathaniel Hawthorne* was torpedoed and sunk in the middle of the night; two hours later the British 5,748 ton steamer *Lindenhall* was similarly accounted for. Ten days later there was an early morning engagement which resulted in another British steamer, the 5,318 ton *City of Corinth*, being torpedoed and sunk. Then, in another ten-day cycle, yet another British steamer was torpedoed and sunk. This time it was the 6,191 ton *Clan MacFadyen* that succumbed just after midnight. On the next night *U-508* struck again, sinking the 5,970 ton British ship *Empire Cromwell*. Just four days later, and in the same area off the coast of British Guiana, Georg Staats struck yet again and two more British ships were lost, the 5,299 ton motor ship *Trevalgan* and the 5,000 ton steamer *City of Bath*. Yet again these were night sinkings and within two hours of each other. Just before midnight the next day, 3 December, yet another British steamer, the 4,561 ton *Solon II* was sent to the bottom. Four days later, this time just after midnight, the 5,423 ton steamer *Nigerian*, another British ship, became the ninth and last victim of the patrol.

By carrying out these night surface attacks Georg Staats was exactly carrying out the instructions laid down in the handbook for U-boat commanders, which read:

Torpedo attack surfaced is only carried out by night. The purpose of attack surfaced, as of attack submerged following the same firing principles, is being unobserved at short range. Do not fire too soon by night, on too fine an inclination. A trainer without sufficient experience is inclined to think the inclination wider than it really is. Keep a cool head, therefore, and do not fire too soon.

The difficulty of seeing the surfaced U-boat by night is due to its low and slender silhouette, since it disappears almost entirely into the water except for the conning tower. The conning tower is more easily recognizable by the enemy at the moment when, according to his height of eye, it is outlined against the horizon. This, therefore, is the danger zone when closing. But when the conning tower has only the surface of the sea for background it is very difficult to distinguish.

Closing from the windward side, proceed with the sea on the quarter so as to reduce the bow wave which is particularly visible in a calm sea. The windward side also offers the advantage of worse observation conditions for the enemy, especially with wind and rain. In no case, when attacking by night, is it permissible to overestimate the enemy's hydrophone listening and allow this consideration to hinder one from making a decisive attack at short range.

Only in rare cases, with a calm sea, and slow speed on the part of the enemy, is there any need to fear that the U-boat will be located by asdic. Conditions are less favourable for locating a surfaced U-boat than a submerged one, owing to the considerable disturbances on the surface, that is continual eddies produced by the sea and by the ship's way. Before submerging or going deep alter course entirely. Remember that the first and most dangerous depth charges will be dropped in a pattern at the diving point and in the direction of the supposed withdrawal.

In war, by night, the better eye and the more attentive look-out will decide between success and failure. The first to see always holds the advantage. By night, therefore, especially during an attack, the look-outs on the bridge must be those with the best night vision. Watch, at night, is kept only with binoculars. In rain or seaway, post a rating in the conning tower to keep dry binoculars ready and to dry the wet ones.

After the sinking of nine ships, it was an elated crew that arrived back at base on 6 January 1943. They were happier still to learn that they would spend six weeks ashore, able to breathe in fresh air twenty-four hours a day!

The next two patrols for *U-508* were not too successful. Leaving its Brittany base on 22 February, the U-boat entered the Bay of Biscay and immediately hit the wild Atlantic tide that swirls in that area of coves and islands. An almost continual procession of Allied aircraft patrolled the Bay but *U-508* escaped their attention until it reached an area north-west of Spain. Here it was attacked and damaged by a Liberator of 224 Squadron operating out of St Eval and had to return to Lorient, arriving on 15 March.

The surprise value which aircraft have by virtue of their high speed, and the large area they could cover for the same reason, compelled the U-boats to keep a constant watch while on the surface. Thus, while within aircraft range, and on the surface, there was a constant strain on the crew and the effect of the air offensive on the morale of a U-boat's crew was tremendous, none more so than when the U-boat had already successfully survived an attack.

At this time attacks on outgoing U-boats were very remunerative. The Allies had realised that under the cloudy conditions of the North Atlantic an aircraft painted pure white was found to offer the nearest appearance to invisibility and therefore all aircraft used exclusively on anti-U-boat operations were so camouflaged.

It was two-and-a-half months before *U-508* was able to put to sea again and therefore it was not involved in the May carnage in which 41 U-boats were sunk and the Atlantic boats were ordered to return to base. When *U-508* sailed on 29 May, it was one of the very few boats outward-bound 'and that was not for long as two days later it returned with a defect.

One week later, and with fingers crossed, Georg Staats successfully left Lorient on what was now *U-508*'s fifth war patrol, its destination the coast of West Africa.

This time the patrol area was reached without too many alarms. The first victim, and the largest, was sunk a month after *U-508* sailed. The French steamer *De la Salle* of 8,400 tons was torpedoed in the Bight of Benin between Accra and Lagos. In the same area, and on the same day, the British 5,343 ton steamer *Manchester Citizen* was similarly torpedoed and sunk. There had been an eight month gap between the last sinkings off the South American seaboard to these off the coast of Togoland. Nine days later, on 18 July, a little to the south of the last attack position and now in the Gulf of Guinea, *U-508* struck again. This time the British 7,369 ton motor vessel *Incomati* became the U-boat's fourteenth, and last, victim when she was torpedoed and sunk. After the sweltering heat of the tropics the crew were pleased when they heard of the recall signal.

The bronzed bodies of *U-508*'s crew emerged from their U-boat when it secured alongside at Lorient on 14 September and went ashore for what, for many of them, would be their last leave. Long leave was granted to the crew and many returned to their homes in Germany.

The boat was transferred to the St Nazaire flotilla and it was from the U-boat pens at this port at the mouth of the river Loire that Georg Staats conned his U-boat out into the basin, through the south lock, out of the Avant port and into the Bay where the tides can at times be deceptively dangerous.

The theatre of operations was to be the Atlantic and *U-508* took the shortest route, travelling midway across the Bay of Biscay, following the 46 degree line. The crossing was safely negotiated and Georg Staats sent a signal to U-boat headquarters on 12 November confirming this. Unfortunately this was as far as the U-boat would reach. At a point north-east of Cape Ortegal the U-boat was caught on the surface by an American Navy Liberator of 103 Squadron operating out of Dunkeswell. The crew of C-Charlie were not to know that earlier in the year *U-508* had been severely shaken up by a Liberator; the U-boat crew were determined they would not be caught a second time and had put in hours of practice to prevent such an eventuality.

The unsuspecting pilot approached the U-boat, dropped his depth charges and at the same time came under fire from the U-boat's armament. The depth charges were on target and so were the U-boat's gunners. What happened in those last few minutes can only be speculation as the Knight's Cross holder and all his crew lost their lives, as did the American airmen. The wreckage of the Liberator and the U-boat now litter the seabed where the Bay of Biscay meets the Atlantic Ocean.

Two days later, on Sunday 14 November, *U-794* a Type XVII boat and the world's first 'true submarine' entered U-boat service at Kiel. This boat was powered by the Walter hydrogen peroxide fuel oil turbine. This was the snorkel type boat for which Admiral Dönitz had high hopes, but the boat's phenomenal performance was marred by serious technical problems that could not be immediately solved. The Type VII and IX boats had to carry on.

The following day the U-boat commander abandoned operations in the Western Atlantic following totally abortive forays on two UK-bound convoys off Newfoundland.

The Liberator aircraft, of which more were built than any other operational aircraft before or since, was becoming a vital factor in the U-boat war. Already two U-boats had been lost for ever in three days, and on 16 November one more was to become another Liberator victim.

This U-boat was *U-280*, a Type VIIC boat launched at the beginning of the year from the Bremer Vulkan yard at Vegesack. The commander, appointed straight from the commanding officers' course at Memel, was Oberleutnant Walter Hungerhausen. This former IWO of *U-128* had left the successful Type IXC boat in mid-February to join the course. His own commanding officer had left *U-128* at the same time and they could both consider themselves fortunate as their former boat became just another statistic when it became one of the 41 U-boat victims sunk in May.

Usually when a prospective commanding officer had completed his course he was appointed to a U-boat type in which he had completed his apprenticeship, but it was not to be for Walter Hungerhausen. He was appointed to the new Type VIIC *U-280*, although he was experienced on the larger Type IXC boat. In *U-128* he was fortunate to have had Kapitänleutnant Ulrich Heyse as his skipper. This 36-year-old commander had been in the merchant service before entering the Kriegsmarine and had the common touch that ingratiated him to his crew. The boat was extremely successful with torpedo and gunfire on its five patrols with Walter Hungerhausen as its IWO, but at the same time experienced depth charge actions at sea and British bombing at Lorient.

The new young commander was hoping to put all that he had learned into practice when he set sail from Kiel on 12 October, his destination the North Atlantic.

It will be remembered that Admiral Dönitz had ordered his U-boats back from off Newfoundland owing to their lack of success in locating UK bound convoys; *U-280* was one of the boats concerned. The new area of operations for Walter Hungerhausen and his crew was to be with a pack of boats to attack homeward-bound convoys to Britain off Gibraltar. Unfortunately for the U-boat, when some six hundred miles north of the Azores and making for its new position, it came quite close to the escorts of an eastbound convoy that the pack had been searching for unsuccessfully. The convoy,

HX265, escorted by the 5th Escort Group, also had the 7th Escort Group in attendance. This convoy was following the route that its two predecessors had taken and the inability of the packs to find them had caused their recall. Now, quite by accident *U-280* had fallen in with its escorts, and was to pay dearly.

On that grey November morning, the 16th, just as it was beginning to get light, the convoy executed an emergency turn to starboard for half-an-hour to dodge any U-boat that might have dived ahead for a dawn attack. As the area ahead of the convoy appeared to be clear of U-boats the 7th Escort Group left their station to sweep down the starboard side and around the stern to where the U-boats could possibly be; both divisions of the 5th Escort Group were already there.

Two Swordfish biplanes from *Biter* were patrolling round the convoy; when the first Liberator arrived at 0845 it was ordered to patrol around the convoy at a radius of forty miles. At 0930 an attack on a U-boat was reported well south of the position.

It must have been at much about this time that *U-280* saw the 5th Escort Group astern of the convoy. At 1000 *Nene* reported attacking a U-boat 24 miles astern of the convoy and *U-280* reported in to U-boat Command. A gnat was heard to explode at the end of its run.

While all this activity was going on Liberator FL931, M-Mother of 86 Squadron was trundling towards the convoy at its most economical speed. The pilot, Flying Officer J. H. Bookless and his crew, had received a very early call as they were airborne from their Irish base of Ballykelly at 0255.

At 1025 a U-boat, *U-280*, was sighted. The aircraft must have been seen at the same time as the U-boat did not have time to dive before the Liberator was upon it. The pilot carried out an immediate attack and the front gunner opened fire and scored hits on the conning tower. The U-boat captain was executing tight turns to port as his gunners were finding the range. Intense and accurate flak was pumped up at the attacker and a shell hit the leading edge of the port wing, putting the port outer engine out of action. The first depth charges overshot and the pilot prepared for another attack. Three minutes later the Liberator came in for a second attempt. In theory the U-boat should have been able to dive in that time, but perhaps encouraged by its first hits, or being aware that it was more dangerous to be hit submerging than submerged, *U-280* remained on the surface. It was to be a fatal miscalculation, for as the Liberator roared in for its second attack the front gunner once more opened fire and this time decimated the gun's crew and scored more hits on the conning tower. The depth charges made a slight overshoot, the nearest estimated to explode thirty feet from the hull. It was enough; a few minutes later *U-280* slowly submerged without any forward movement and it was never to be seen again. The pilot circled the position but despite remaining in the vicinity for one-and-three quarter hours saw no evidence of destruction, but *U-280* had sunk with the loss of all its crew.

The VLR Liberator III finally reached Ballykelly on three engines at 2012 after seventeen hours fifteen minutes eventful airborne patrolling. The convoy it was escorting arrived at the Clyde on the 19th, unscathed.

The next U-boat victim to be sunk at sea was also an aircraft victim. Among the No 179 Squadron pilots living in spartan conditions at the Lagens airfield, on the island of Terceira in the Azores, was Flying Officer D. F. McRae, the holder of the Distinguished Flying Cross. The airmen, with their Leigh light Wellingtons, had been on the Portuguese island for less than a month and the only facilities that were available for their night flying role were a hurricane lamp flarepath and a Chance light. There were also two Sandra lights on top of the north-east ridge level with the end of the runway, and a third on the north-east coast.

At night the Leigh light Wellingtons took over the convoy escort from the day squadrons. On the evening of 18 November Flying Officer McRae and his crew of F-Freddie were briefed to carry out an anti-U-boat patrol over convoy SL139/MKS30. Taking off from their lava dust runway, which formed over a porous stone base, the Wellington was airborne just over an hour before midnight. It was a dark night, but the aircraft's navigation was spot on and the Wellington met the convoy after three-and-a-quarter hours in the air. At this time the convoy was making steady progress northwards some 450 miles west-south-west of Cape Finisterre.

When the convoy was first located it was too dark for the navigator to check its speed and course.

Down below, also looking for the convoy was Kapitänleutnant Karl Hause, commanding his Type VIIC boat *U-211*. Before commencing its fifth operational patrol between Spain and the Azores, *U-211* had been fitted out as a flak boat, and should have been well capable of protecting itself against air attack. The boat had been built by the Germania Werft at Kiel and launched some twenty months earlier. Its initial cruise was cut short at Arendal. The first war cruise was from Bergen to the Atlantic on 26 August 1942.

The first patrol was to be its most successful. On 12 September *U-211* penetrated the convoy ranks of ON127 and fired two torpedoes into the 13,797 ton *Hektoria* and another into the 6,849 ton *Empire Moonbeam*. Both these British ships sank when given the *coup de grâce* later by *U-608*. Eleven days later *U-211* torpedoed and sank the American 11,237 ton tanker *Esso Williamsburg*. It was an elated crew that put into its new base at Brest on 6 October.

After sampling the delights of north-western France for six weeks *U-211* was back at sea, on a North Atlantic patrol. This time the target was convoy ON153. *U-211* did not sink any merchantmen but sank HMS *Firedrake*, a Royal Navy destroyer that had recently been repaired in the United States after sustaining aerial damage while escorting a convoy to Malta. Indeed this was the last success for *U-211*. The next patrol, in mid-February, was aborted when the U-boat returned to Brest after twelve days suffering from damage inflicted by the USAAF No 1 composite squadron.

The U-boat survived the May 1943 holocaust and left in the middle of the month to patrol well south-west of the Azores; it returned two months later with no successes to report.

After being fitted as a flak boat *U-211* was back at sea on 14 October. A month later, in mid-afternoon of 16 November, U-boat headquarters issued orders for nine U-boats to be in position to intercept the convoy; *U-211* was one of them. It was exactly within the area ordered when located by F-Freddie.

The Wellington carried out a creeping line search on reaching the convoy and after ninety minutes, while flying at 1,000 feet some fifty miles to the east of the ships, an ASV contact was made to port at a range of three miles. The Wellington turned to port and down below a U-boat, *U-211*, was seen in the moonlight, fully surfaced. Because the noise of the U-boat's diesels blotted out the sound of the aircraft's engines the bridge watch did not hear the Wellington and the pilot wisely decided not to use his Leigh light immediately as it was obvious that the U-boat had not seen him or it would have opened fire. It was hoped to catch the U-boat by surprise. The attack was made at 90 degrees to port of the U-boat's track. The U-boat was making 5 to 8 knots through the water as the depth charges were dropped thirty feet aft of its bow, two to port, and two to starboard. As the depth charges straddled *U-211* the aircraft's front gunner fired a few rounds and two bursts of orange-coloured flak shot out from the guns aft of the conning tower. The U-boat became enveloped in depth charge plumes as the second and third charges exploded. From above the rear gunner saw two bright blue flames which appeared to come from amidships. On signalling base the Wellington pilot was told to remain on convoy patrol until relieved by a Fortress.

The rest of the patrol was carried out without further incident and after nearly eleven hours in the air Flying Officer McRae came in at sea level, lifting his Wellington up over the coastline between the two ridges, put his undercarriage down and landed on the Lagens runway. After taxiing the Wellington to dispersal near the red-tiled stone administration buildings, the tired crew reported to the Intelligence officer.

Although it was thought fairly certain that *U-211* had been sunk, the same crew took another Wellington XIV, C-Charlie, out the next day to search the area for tracks which might have been made by a damaged U-boat. They need not have bothered. Kapitänleutnant Karl Hause and all his crew in *U-211* had perished in the night attack. The Wellington had been the first aircraft from the Azores to sink an enemy by night and the pilot by his surprise attack had not given the U-boat's gunners enough time to make use of their superior gun armament.

The position of *U-211*, being exactly where it was ordered to be, but fifty miles east of the convoy confirms that U-boat intercepts were made and that the convoy had been diverted westwards to avoid the waiting pack.

CHAPTER THREE

A Very Special Operation

Rolf Schauenburg was born in the Swiss town of Winterthur at the end of May 1913. As a twenty-year-old he joined the Kriegsmarine and was in the 1934 class. He was appointed to the old battleship *Schlesien*, launched in 1906 which the Germans had been allowed to retain after the Kaiser's war. Although the old battleship was used mainly for cadet training duties it did attend the 1937 Spithead naval review to celebrate the Coronation of King George VI and Queen Elizabeth. Rolf Schauenburg was aboard but he later transferred to *Graf Spee*, another Kriegsmarine ship that attended the review.

Rolf Schauenburg was still serving, as a gunnery officer, aboard the pocket battleship, when together with her sister ship *Deutschland*, she left Wilhelmshaven towards the end of August 1939 to be in position before war was declared. The pocket battleships' respective supply ships *Altmark* and *Westerwald* had preceded them, and were waiting on station in the Atlantic ready to replenish them.

Graf Spee left Germany unreported, hugged the coast of Norway and reached the North Atlantic unobserved and rendezvoused with *Altmark* to take on fuel on 1 September. Once war had officially been declared two days later *Graf Spee* sailed west to the eastern coast of Brazil, bent on destruction and disruption. In the meantime one of Schauenburg's former ships, had fired the first naval shots of the war, in Baltic operations, against Poland. Now, his present ship was to fire the first salvoes on commerce raiding in the Atlantic.

The first merchantman was sunk on the last day of the month and by mid-December the total of ships lost to the Allies had risen to nine as Kapitän Langsdorff skilfully kept his pocket battleship unobserved as he traversed east and west across the South Atlantic picking off ships steaming alone. Many prisoners were taken and most of them were offloaded on to *Altmark* which soon acquired a reputation as a notorious prison ship. On 13 December an uneven battle between *Graf Spee* and HM cruisers *Exeter, Ajax* and *Achilles*, known as the Battle of the River Plate took place off Montevideo. After battle damage the German warship arrived at the neutral Uruguayan port for repairs. All the remaining prisoners and many of the crew were landed. *Graf Spee* left after four days and promptly scuttled herself. The crew were interned and three days later the captain took his life. Rolf Schauenburg managed to get himself interned, on the other side of the River Plate, by the Argentinians.

The German internee escaped from his captors and represented himself as a cloth dealer; he spoke English and Spanish fluently. He was twice arrested but at this time Argentina was pro-German and as he had influential friends in the South American country he was released. After a year away from the war he returned to Germany at the beginning of 1941. Following leave, Rolf Schauenburg was glad to be back in uniform again and was appointed to the minesweeper *M31*. After a while he was given a task interrogating British prisoners of war, and then transferred to the U-boat arm. After training he served in the Atlantic as a watch officer to Kapitänleutnant Heinz-Otto Schultze aboard the successful *U-432* for three months. After further training, including a commanding officer's course, Rolf Schauenburg was appointed commander of *U-536* at the beginning of 1943 with the rank of Kapitänleutnant. The Type IXC$_{40}$ boat had been launched at the Deutsche Werke, in Hamburg, three months earlier.

˙ Two days after his thirtieth birthday Kapitänleutnant Rolf Schauenburg conned his first command out of Kiel on its first war cruise. Its destination was the Azores area; it will be remembered that Admiral Dönitz had recalled all his North and Mid-Atlantic boats back to their Biscay bases a week earlier, after the terrible losses in May.

U-536 had scarcely passed the Rosengarten, the bank thirty miles in radius between the Faroes and Iceland, when it was ordered to a refuelling area south of the Azores. Its sister U-boat *U-535* and *U-170*, also Type IXC$_{40}$ boats, received the same instructions. All three boats had to discharge their fuel to five other boats. The

waiting boats had been beleaguered by the events of May when their
refuelling boats had been sunk.

After the successful transfer the three boats, *U-170*, *U-535* and
U-536, were ordered to proceed to Lorient to have new anti-aircraft
equipment fitted before setting out on offensive patrols. Towards the
end of June the three U-boats set course for the Biscay base. They
approached the Bay of Biscay from due west, intending to pass close to
the north of Cape Finisterre, then for a short time hug the coast of
Spain before turning to the north-eastwards and base. However,
before they had even reached the perimeter of the Bay they had been
attacked by aircraft three times. The first two attacks were ineffective
but not so the third, carried out by a Liberator of No 53 Squadron.
This attack, on 5 July, with the U-boats surfaced and keeping a good
lookout, saw them in formation, with Rolf Schauenburg as senior
officer leading in *U-536* with *U-535* on its port quarter and *U-170*
astern. The submariners were hoping that their luck would hold as in
the previous two attacks. It didn't. Although it was early evening there
was still plenty of summer daylight as G-George of 53 Squadron
spotted the trio below. As the Liberator came in the first time his attack
was defeated by the successful avoiding action of the U-boats; in the
second attack the depth charges failed to release but the aircraft's
gunners peppered the bridge crew of *U-536*.

Although no charges were dropped the attack was so determined,
intense and accurate that Rolf Schauenburg decided to dive
immediately before the aircraft could get into position for a further
attempt. Instructions were given to the other boats to dive. As the air
hissed from its tanks the crew of *U-536* heard the unmistakable sound
of depth charges detonating; the depth charges were released at the
third attempt. Eight charges straddled *U-535*, which had been slow to
submerge, possibly because of damage it had received when attacked
passing through the Rosengarten earlier.

Prudently waiting five hours until darkness had set in, before
surfacing, the two surviving boats searched unavailingly for any signs
of Oberleutnant Ellmanreich or his crew, but all had perished in
U-535. The news had a sobering effect on the two crews as they
proceeded on the dangerous last leg to base, which they reached safely
on 9 July.

A crew member of *U-536* tells the story of the attack from his angle:

We were one of three boats, we were with *U-170* and *U-535*. *U-535* was one of our boats; we completed at the same time as they did because we got through the tactical exercises more quickly. Then there was *U-170*, a Bremen boat. We were sailing in the middle; the three boats were sailing through the Bay of Biscay on the surface; *U-170* was sailing on the right and *U-535* on the left. Then there was a Liberator, they are frightful things. We took evasive action, we kept turning and the commander kept calling out, 'Hard a-starboard!, Hard a-port!' He was damned smart. Missed every time. He passed over us dead astern at a height of fifty metres I should say. Bomb doors open, but no bombs dropped. The Commander called, 'Hard a-starboard', we turned hard a-starboard, showed the red flag for submerging and immediately went in to a crash dive, and *U-170* submerged too. We listened and heard depth charges dropped by the aircraft; then we heard no more. We surfaced again, but before that we had remained submerged for five or six hours. We sailed back and surfaced again at the same spot to see if we could find anything, patches of oil or something, we didn't find anything. So only two of us put in to port. The other one got it in the neck during its first patrol.

Kapitänleutnant Rolf Schauenburg was different from most U-boat commanders in that he brought to *U-536* the standards of a battleship; thus although the custom was for U-boat crews to return from patrol hirsute and grimy the only time his U-boat came into Lorient his men were all freshly washed and shaved.

Lorient was known as 'the base of the aces'. Günther Prien, Joachim Schepke and Otto Kretschmer had all operated from the French base. While Rolf Schauenburg had been at sea in *Graf Spee* Günther Prien had hit the world's headlines with his daring foray into Scapa Flow, in October 1939 to sink the British battleship *Royal Oak*. Then, with the other two commanders, he caused havoc in the Atlantic attacking merchant shipping. The three, together with the other U-boat commanders, were implementing the wolf pack technique of warfare instituted by their leader, Admiral Dönitz. This tactic involved a sighting U-boat resisting the temptation of attacking the convoy alone, but reporting and tracking the convoy until headquarters could bring sufficient numbers of other boats in the pack to inflict losses out of all proportion to their own numbers. The *Rudelsystem*, with several U-boats attacking simultaneously, stretched the convoy escort vessels beyond their limited resources. By the end of February 1941 Prien, Schepke and Kretschmer had all sunk over 200,000 tons of Allied shipping and in Germany they were fêted, decorated and treated as national heroes.

At the end of February the three aces were back at sea. They enjoyed their friendly rivalry; in fact they had made a pact that the first one to sink 300,000 tons of shipping would be given a night out paid for by the other two; it was not to be. There was filthy weather as the aces slipped their moorings at Lorient and headed back to the convoy routes in their Type VIIB boats, none would return. On 10 March Prien and all his crew in *U-47* were sunk by the destroyer HMS *Wolverine*.

On the evening of 15 March *U-99* and *U-100*, with Kretschmer and Schepke, were ordered to a position to intercept convoy HX112, which had been reported by the notorious Fritz Lemp who on the opening day of the war had torpedoed the passenger liner *Athenia*. 'Silent Otto' Kretschmer had already whetted his appetite by sinking a 20,000 ton whaling factory ship a week earlier. On reaching the convoy, *U-99* wasted no time and sank six of the ships, but the next day, St Patrick's Day, was to see the destruction of both *U-99* and *U-100*. The latter was damaged by depth charges and attempting to escape on the surface was rammed by HMS *Vanoc*. Joachim Schepke lost his life and only five of the crew were rescued.

The last of the trio, *U-99*, was on the surface when sighted by a destroyer. The watch officer on the bridge decided to dive. A pattern of depth charges rained down and the U-boat was so damaged that it was forced to surface. Otto Kretschmer was first out of the conning tower and saw a destroyer, *Vanoc*, which had been damaged by ramming *U-100*. Unfortunately for him he was out of torpedoes. Another destroyer, HMS *Walker*, with bow waves breaking over the deck was speeding to the scene and together both destroyers opened up with light and heavy armament. None of the U-boat's crew would have had a chance to reach the guns without being mown down. There was only one choice left; scuttle the boat. The crew were ordered to put on their warmest clothing and the hatches were opened; *U-99* sank stern first. Otto Kretschmer and all except three of his crew were taken prisoner on board *Walker*.

Within a week U-boat command had lost their three best known U-boats and two of their commanders; Otto Kretschmer alone survived to become a prisoner of war.

After being landed at Liverpool the prize capture was whisked to London for interrogation. His captors learned nothing new, Kretschmer was not known as 'Silent Otto' for no reason! He was later taken to an officers' camp in the Lake District where he was senior officer; his appointment to Korvettenkapitän had been promulgated on 1 March. Through a pre-arranged code he was able, using next-of-kin cards, to let U-boat headquarters know what had happened.

A year later, in May 1942, Kretschmer and other U-boat officers were told that they were being transferred to Canada. The thought of a voyage across the Atlantic at the mercy of marauding U-boats filled them with foreboding. However, the ocean crossing was safely completed and the prisoners entrained for Bowmanville Camp, located near Lake Ontario. The conditions and food were better than those enjoyed in England and throughout 1942 Americans of German origin supplied comforts to the prisoners of war.

Although conditions were much improved Kretschmer and several other U-boat officers badly wanted their freedom and resolved to try to escape and return to Germany. This naturally was a long term plan and required a great deal of organisation; should it succeed and U-boat commanders of the calibre of Kretschmer return to Germany the propaganda value to Doctor Goebbels would be enormous and the lift to morale of U-boat men everywhere would be incalculable. Admiral Dönitz needed all the U-boat commanders he could muster and experienced ones were priceless.

The long term plan formulated was that a secret tunnel be built, Kretschmer, his 1WO and two other U-boat commanders would escape and make for the eastern seaboard where they would be picked up by a U-boat.

Although success might have appeared highly improbable when they started, the inhabitants of Bowmanville worked with a high resolve. Tunnels and dummy tunnels were dug; through a correspondence with his 1WO's mother U-boat headquarters were kept informed.

While talking of watch officers it might be appropriate here to

mention some who served with Otto Kretschmer and inherited some
of his ideas. There was Hans Dietrich Freiherr von Tiesenhausen
who later, as commander of *U-331*, sank the only British battleship
to be sunk at sea in the Second World War, when he torpedoed
Barham in the Mediterranean in November 1941. There was another
Baron, Siegfried von Forstner; with *U-402* in its two years at sea he
sank sixteen Allied ships to become the twelfth most successful U-
boat captain. Then there was Klaus Bargsten, who sank the famous
British destroyer HMS *Cossack* and other ships. For operations in
U-563 and *U-521* he, like the other two commanders mentioned,
was awarded the Knight's Cross.

Now, in Canada, Otto Kretschmer's last 1WO, Knebel-Döberitz,
was communicating through his mother and U-boat headquarters
about escaping with Kretschmer, Oberleutnant Elfe, commander of
U-93, another former watch officer in *U-99*, and Hans Ey,
commander of *U-433*. Calculations were made and it was
considered that if everything continued to work smoothly, though
allowing a margin of error for unforeseen circumstances, the
provisional date for escape would be somewhere after mid-
September. This was communicated to U-boat headquarters.

Although Karl Dönitz had been appointed head of the
Kriegsmarine at the beginning of 1943 he still kept his finger very
much on the pulse of the U-boat arm. Despite his overall
responsibility of running Hitler's fleet he was still close to his U-boat
crews, and affectionately known as 'Uncle Karl'. When he heard
that *U-536* had safely berthed at Lorient he knew he had his man.
Work was put in hand to supply the new anti-aircraft armament and
then Rolf Schauenburg was summoned to Grand Admiral Dönitz's
headquarters near Berlin. The U-boat commander was a
determined character after the Admiral's own heart. It was an
inspirational choice by the head of the Kriegsmarine. A U-boat
commander that had been an internee on a hostile continent,
appreciating the problems and despair of a prisoner would surely be
the right man to cross the ocean to rescue Germany's ace U-boat
commander. As an added bonus Schauenburg spoke English well.

The rescue operation was over two months away, so Admiral
Dönitz did not give Rolf Schauenburg the full details, for the fewer
people that knew the less likelihood there was that something would

go wrong. Whatever passed between Dönitz and Schauenburg, the latter did not take his crew into his confidence, and, when they sailed on 29 August they had no idea that they were to undertake a special operation. This was no doubt accounted for by the fact that at the time of sailing Schauenburg did not know for certain that he would be going to Canada. Before he was clear of the Bay, however, he received word that he was to open his sealed orders and special codes. Schauenburg called his men together and gave them an outline of the operation. He told his officers that communication was to be established with the escaping prisoners by wireless and showed them the detailed charts of the area in which the rendezvous had been fixed: Chaleur Bay.

The U-boat entered the Gulf of St Lawrence on 16 September, and had a week or ten days in which to perfect its arrangements. The 2WO and a stoker were to go ashore in a dinghy specially fitted with an outboard motor. The former, a young man of twenty, was looking forward to the adventure and employed himself in preparing a special 'gangster's cap.' It looked like an ordinary cap but the peak was loaded with lead and, if he was accosted by anyone ashore, he was going to take it off politely – and then hit the man in the face with it.

Schauenburg had been ordered to be in Chaleur Bay by 26 September, but actually arrived there two or three days earlier. It was as well that he had, for he found that his charts were not up to date; the section of the rendezvous was partly to be fixed by reference to a solitary house and, in the area where the solitary house was supposed to be, he could see only a cluster of buildings. He spent several hours spying out the land through his periscope and with some difficulty found the correct rendezvous.

Meanwhile all was going well at the camp. The tunnel was over 100 yards long, but on the very day Kretschmer and the other three had decided to escape the tunnel roof collapsed just by the camp perimeter. A keen gardener among the prisoners decided he wanted some top soil and had the shock of his life when his spade broke through into the shaft. This was seen by the guards and the tunnel was soon found. Nearly a year's work by 150 prisoners had been lost.

Hiding his disappointment Otto Kretschmer saw it as his duty to try to contact the waiting U-boat so that it would not itself be endangered. There was an attempt to contact the boat by radio, and the next evening, 24 September, Kapitänleutnant Heyda staged a daring break-out over the wire to the rendezvous to the north of the mouth of the St Lawrence. His disappearance was concealed from the camp authorities as he travelled eastwards by train, towards the coast. Eventually arriving at the meeting place, he was disappointed to find a small detachment of Canadian warships. Before he could reach the shore the former commander of *U-434* was surrounded by an Army patrol for being in a prohibited area. The German successfully bluffed the patrol and was released with a warning to keep away from the area.

The following night Heyda was captured as he tried to reach a beach. This time the game was up and he was detained. It was now 27 September.

Out at sea *U-536* had picked up a signal which was thought to have been transmitted by the prisoners, but it was not repeated. The night before Otto Kretschmer and his companions were due to arrive Schauenburg decided to leave the Bay and stand out into the Gulf where he could give his batteries a good charge. Just before he dived, he sighted a destroyer and a corvette; to seaward there were half a dozen more vessels. Schauenburg remained stopped at periscope depth and watched them. He saw the corvette take up her position near the rendezvous; after some hours she was relieved by another.

Throughout the next day the U-boat lay on the bottom of Chaleur Bay. Schauenburg decided that to attempt to carry out his order was hopeless; all that he could do now was to get his U-boat safely out of the Bay. When it was dark, he crept out into the St Lawrence, keeping at about 65 feet. He could hear the ships moving about the Bay; at one time he found that he was being followed but after a little while the ship altered course and, though depth charges were dropped, they were some distance away.

On reaching the open sea, Schauenburg made for the Cabot Strait. There he sighted a destroyer apparently alone, and fired a salvo of three torpedoes. All of them missed. From the Cabot Strait the boat proceeded to the Halifax area, where it patrolled for nearly a month. A good deal of shipping was sighted but somehow the commander never managed to get into an attacking position. It was not until 12 October that a sinking was claimed, a Liberty ship of over 10,000 tons. Unfortunately no Allied ship had been sunk. Four electric torpedoes were fired in two salvoes without result and it was thought that they had hit without exploding. A fifth torpedo was then fired without finding its mark. Two more ships were attacked, one of them said to be a liner of over 20,000 tons and the other a small merchantman. Against the liner two air torpedoes were used and against the merchantman two electric, but the result was the same in both cases – a miss.

About the middle of November, Schauenburg requested permission to return from patrol as his fuel was running low, and received orders to return to Lorient. No doubt if the mission had been successful and the prisoners rescued the boat would have returned immediately keeping away from the usual convoy lines to ensure the safety of the important personages.

On 18 November *U-536* was told that it was to take advantage of any opportunity to attack a convoy that a pack of other boats was concentrating on and Schauenburg complied although at the time he had only 30 tons of fuel remaining in his bunkers.

We will follow the later progress of *U-536* in the next chapter.

CHAPTER FOUR

Convoy Targets

The convoy that *U-536* had been directed to was SL139/MKS30. German agents watching movements off Gibraltar had reported the imminent departure of that part of the convoy on 13 November. The SL139 half had sailed up from West Africa. After joining forces at midday on 14th, all was organised and the ships departed from the assembly point off Cape St Vincent two-and-a-half hours later. The combined convoy consisting of 67 ships, including eleven LSTs, was ranged in fourteen columns with HMS *Ranpura* in company. The escort was provided by EG40 comprising HM ships *Exe*, *Milford*, *Moyola*, *Clarkia*, *Petunia* and *Kistna*, with the senior officer in *Exe*.

Two days later *Ranpura* and a merchantman were detached to return to Gibraltar independently. That same day, and the next afternoon, a Focke Wulf Condor was observed circling the convoy for half-an-hour.

In the early hours of the 18th a Wellington of 172 Squadron sighted a fully surfaced U-boat 270 miles ahead of the convoy. A full pattern of depth charges was dropped but no reports of damage were intercepted.

Acting on information from the Condor, U-boat headquarters ordered a line of U-boats to form across the convoy's path. *U-426*, *U-262*, *U-228*, *U-515*, *U-358*, *U-333*, *U-211* and *U-600* formed this first, southernmost, line.

U-536, returning from its mission off the St Lawrence and two U-boats homeward bound from the Caribbean area were told of the convoy's position and ordered to take advantage of any opportunity to attack. Later that morning U-boat control estimated the convoy to be 80 miles south-east of the line and the eight U-boats were

50

ordered to travel submerged, at three knots, to what was hoped would be the correct intercept position during the night.

Although nothing had been picked up on H/F D/F by the ships or their escorts Kapitänleutnant Ali Cremer in his Type VIIC *U-333* found himself in position, within striking distance in the late morning. First two of the escorts and then the convoy were seen. His tubes were ready loaded to fire, but his periscope was seen from *Exe* and depth charges came raining down. Shortly afterwards the U-boat scraped the destroyer's bottom with its periscope, causing the periscope to break off. The U-boat immediately flooded and rapidly went into an uncontrolled dive. Gradually equilibrium was restored and the boat righted itself, but it was badly damaged. The U-boat commander, who had already sunk a freighter on this patrol, was left reflecting on what might have been as he heard the propeller screws from the convoy passing above. His more immediate problem was that of saving his boat and getting a message through to headquarters reporting the position of the convoy. Unfortunately for U-boat headquarters the U-boat's wireless transmitter had been damaged and only a garbled message was received.

Early in the afternoon three ships of the 7th Escort Group joined to reinforce the escort; HM ships *Pheasant*, *Crane* and *Chanticleer*. Other escort forces were to join later and as Senior Officer, *Pheasant* was ordered to take charge of all support forces as they arrived. The senior officer of the main escort group requested that *Chanticleer* sweep to visibility distance, seeking the U-boat attacked by *Exe*. Just over an hour later the sloop reported sighting a U-boat, which dived immediately. This was *U-515*, and its diving position was 25 miles astern of the convoy. *Crane* was then detached to join the hunt. Visibility was ten to fifteen miles and the sloops searched together. An hour later *Chanticleer* reported seeing a periscope a mile ahead. Ten depth charges were ordered to be primed with shallow settings as the asdic picked up the contact. The echo was held as the sloop threw off the first pattern of charges, but already Kapitänleutnant Henke in the U-boat had fired a gnat and a heavy explosion in the stern shook the ship as the homing torpedo found its mark. Both engines and the steering gear were out of action. A second explosion sent a column of water into the air but the sloop suffered no further damage. At this time *U-515* was unaware of the damage it had caused, reporting an unsuccessful attack and that it was damaged from the resulting counter attack. Up above *Crane* had obtained a firm asdic contact at a mile distance eighteen minutes after the torpedoing and for the next two hours carried out six ten-pattern attacks. *U-515* released SBT's but *Crane* held the contact.

Forty minutes later, when the sea had calmed after the last upheaval, the damaged *Chanticleer*, about four miles to the south, picked up an asdic contact at 1,500 yards. *Crane* closed at full speed to the position indicated by the vulnerable sloop. At 800 yards contact was obtained and another pattern of charges dropped. Contact was then lost so *Crane* circled *Chanticleer*, which was then being taken in tow by the rescue tug from the convoy.

The damaged sloop made for the Azores at four knots and successfully reached her new destination. Ironically *U-515* also chose the same area in which to carry out repairs and was therefore out of the firing line. Just to tidy up the day, *U-333* finally got through a report to U-boat headquarters after midnight reporting its damage and saying it was making for base. The badly damaged U-boat finally reached La Pallice at daybreak on 1 December.

HM ships *Foley* and *Garlies* joined the convoy escort but the latter was ordered to screen *Chanticleer*.

U-boat control hoped that the night would bring success, shadowing aircraft would drop light buoys which would indicate the convoy's course. Unfortunately all was not well as the convoy was steaming fifty miles to the west of where the ships were expected. From dusk the aircraft began making beacon signals. *U-262* reported seeing the signals and two hours later also reported starshells. An hour before midnight the damaged *U-515*, moving off from the battle area, reported the convoy's position.

Of the first line of U-boats only *U-333* and *U-515* had been involved. It is worth noting here that the commanders of these two U-boats, Ali Cremer and Werner Henke, were the most experienced captains still at sea; both had been waging the U-boat war for over two years.

Perhaps realising that it was only these captains that were taking calculated risks to reach the convoy and their escorts while the other commanders were showing little spirit, Dönitz exhorted U-boats to get in and 'Kill them'.

HMS *Exe* . . . and (*below*) the view of it seen through *U-333's* periscope

On receipt of *U-515*'s message a second, more northerly, line consisting of *U-709, U-969, U-343, U-586, U-648, U-238, U-618* and *U-86* was ordered to be in position by dusk on the 19th as it was realised that the convoy had passed line 1 to the westward. One U-boat which had been in line 1, *U-426*, was given freedom of action in the area of the line, and *U-608*, who had been unable to join the original line as was intended, was also ordered into the second line.

Before daybreak the convoy had executed a turn to starboard but then aircraft sweeping ahead reported that U-boats were probably on this new track and two alterations were made to bring the ships back on their original course.

Meanwhile HMC ship *Calgary*, with HMCS *Snowberry* in company, joining from the northward, reported two U-boats a hundred miles ahead of the convoy. Almost certainly one of these was *U-648* which reported being attacked by surface forces and that it would have difficulty in reaching the line. The corvettes reported that one U-boat had made off at high speed on the surface while the other dived. An unsuccessful search was carried out before both shaped to join the convoy.

The 5th Escort Group, comprising *Nene*, *Tweed*, *Lunenburg* and *Edmundston*, with *Essington* of the 7th Escort Group in company, also effected a rendezvous in the forenoon. Two of these Canadian corvettes were soon to show their mettle.

Half-an-hour after the 5th and 7th Escort Groups had taken up their day stations respectively on the port and starboard sides of the extended screen *Foley* reported a shadowing Focke Wulf Condor which circled the convoy until chased off by an escorting Flying Fortress. U-boats' attention was drawn to the importance of reporting the shadower's bearings, and it was probably a U-boat so employed that was located by another Fortress in the afternoon 28 miles on the convoy's starboard bow; it prudently dived before an attack could be carried out. The 7th Escort Group went to investigate but found nothing.

U-boats were informed it was essential to report shadowers' positions as they were of decisive importance for the success of the operation. In the early evening the line, with the exception of *U-238, U-618* and *U-86*, were ordered to proceed on course at 13 knots. From this time onwards U-boats began reporting the shadowers' bearings, seven reports were made and this presumably led Control to halt the line at 1930 in the position reached and to order 'Go for it at maximum speed'.

On the surface, bearings began to pour in from ahead of the convoy, so *Nene*, *Calgary* and *Snowberry* were ordered to sweep ahead. The escort was further reinforced by the arrival of *Watchman* and *Winchelsea*. They were stationed on the starboard bow of the extended screen and became part of the 7th Escort Group. Shortly afterwards, it was thought advisable to have an escort stationed on the extended screen astern as two or three H/F D/F bearings had been obtained in that direction; therefore *Foley* was ordered to take up station at a distance of eight miles.

Milford, on the starboard bow of the close screen, obtained an asdic contact on *U-586*. She attacked with ten depth charges but could not regain contact and was ordered to resume station.

Four reports of starshell and three reports of hydrophone bearings were made to U-boat headquarters during the evening. All of these indicated with considerable accuracy that the convoy was due south of the line. The U-boats' prospects should therefore have been good. At this juncture the U-boats of line 1 were told to operate against the convoy as far as position allowed, otherwise they were to remain in the area and await orders. Two of the U-boats did in fact report escort vessels and hydrophone bearings but that was the limit of their achievements.

Some of the starshell reported had been fired from *Nene*, sweeping ahead of the convoy; she had picked up a radar contact at 4,400 yards and increased speed to 19 knots and gave chase. The range did not appear to close so *Nene* opened with starshell; this revealed the fully surfaced *U-238* proceeding at high speed and endeavouring to keep stern on to the pursuing ship. *Nene* maintained a position on its quarter and opened fire, forcing the U-boat to dive. The frigate employed anti-gnat tactics and then closed the diving position which was about 32 miles ahead of the convoy. *Nene* obtained asdic contact and ordered *Calgary* and *Snowberry* to sweep round the position which was marked by a flare. *Nene* ran in to attack and fired her hedgehog but without result. At this time *Watchman* joined but only remained for about half-an-hour before being ordered to rejoin the convoy.

After the hedgehog attack *Nene* regained contact with the U-boat

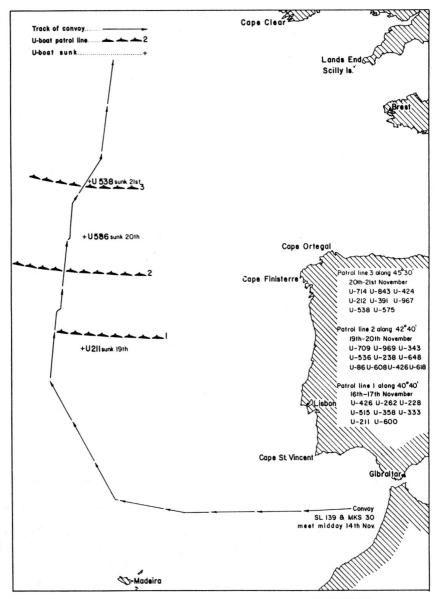

Track of convoy........ ——————➤
U-boat patrol line........ ⬦— ⬦— ⬦ 2
U-boat sunk.................................+

Cape Clear

Lands End
Scilly Is.

Brest

+U 538 sunk 21st
3

+U 586 sunk 20th

Cape Ortegal

Cape Finisterre

Patrol line 3 along 45°30'
20th-21st November
U-714 U-843 U-424
U-212 U-391 U-967
U-538 U-575

Patrol line 2 along 42°40'
19th-20th November
U-709 U-969 U-343
U-536 U-238 U-648
U-86 U-608 U-426 U-618

2

+U 211 sunk 19th

Patrol line 1 along 40°40'
16th-17th November
U-426 U-262 U-228
U-515 U-358 U-333
U-211 U-600

Lisbon

Cape St. Vincent

Gibraltar

Convoy
SL 139 & MKS 30
meet midday 14th Nov.

Madeira

U-boat dispositions for intercepting convoy SL139/MKS30

which had now gone deeper and attacked with a ten charge pattern. Firm contact could not be re-established after this attack so the two corvettes were ordered to extend the legs of the search to six miles. Just before midnight *Snowberry* obtained an asdic contact and attacked with depth charges. *Nene* closed the position; *Snowberry* lost contact astern but picked it up again and made a further attack with ten depth charges. Three marked underwater explosions were heard about three minutes after the attack. Contact was then lost so a search was re-organised round the position of the last attack.

The three ships of the 5th Escort Group were continuing their search, when, at 0052, *Nene* picked up at 700 yards what was thought to be a different contact; this was immediately classified as a U-boat. A flare was then dropped and the new datum point signalled to the corvettes. This position was about sixteen miles ahead of the convoy. *Nene* then opened the range and attacked with a deep pattern. This attack blew the U-boat to the surface and it was at once met with a hail of gunfire by all three ships.

The U-boat was *U-536*, returning from its unfortunate mission to the Canadian coast. It had closed the convoy some 36 hours earlier and had been detected on the surface but it escaped without damage from the attack which followed.

Before *Nene* located *U-536*, the U-boat had had *U-238* on its port beam and the crew had heard the noise of the starshells being fired followed by the sound of the U-boat diving. Then came the detonations of depth charges. These various sounds did not trouble the crew of *U-536* overmuch. Their boat was over 500 feet deep and it seemed pretty certain that *U-238* was getting the benefit of it all; suddenly however the 'ping' of asdics broke in on these comfortable thoughts and before the men knew where they were a pattern of depth charges had descended upon them.

The attack was so sudden and unexpected that it threw them into confusion. It was also so accurate that the crew thought that the charges contained a new explosive. The boat went badly down by the stern, though there was apparently no entry of water. The engineering officer spent an hour endeavouring to regain trim; when at last he gave up his efforts and reported his failure to the commander, the order to surface was given.

While *U-536* was surfacing, the men assembled in the control room in readiness to abandon ship. Under heavy fire from the three ships most of them made good their escape in dinghies, though a direct hit on the conning tower caused some casualties.

Before a boarding party could be got away *U-536* sank stern first, all its vents had been opened and it ran for a short distance under port helm and then sank quickly by the stern at about 0245.

Thirteen survivors were then picked up and, later, the commander, Rolf Schauenburg, and three others were rescued by *Tweed* rejoining from her previous hunt. The patrol, which had begun with such exciting things as sealed orders and a rendezvous in a remote bay, had ended disappointingly. Admiral Dönitz had not only the bad news that Kretschmer had not been rescued but the boat that had been sent for him was now itself sunk.

As the convoy plodded on towards the British Isles, the escorts ever vigilant, one of the engine room ratings from *U-536* remembers the last fateful minutes aboard the U-boat:

Five patterns of depth charges had come down, then one of the old sort of depth charges, which didn't go so deep; the lights went out, everything rattled, the valves flew all over the place. Suddenly we went down by the stern, then 'bump', we heard another charge. I clung on to the rear door of the torpedo tube, just about in the middle of the bow compartment. I looked down and some damned tool box came shooting past my head, then something happened to the hydroplane motor. There was a sound of bubbles and a whole lot of air escaped. The control room was rung up, then the hydroplane was switched over to hand control and the control room took it over. I thought that water was coming in; certainly the bilge water came up and all the deck plates were moving up and down. Everything went aft, all the bilge, the crates, all the deck plates, they all crashed aft. I thought 'My God, we're going down'. I seized a lamp and went aft to the tube and inspected everything. It was all watertight. I sent through a message confirming this, then came the order 'Blow the tanks!' I heard air going into the tanks. Then came a further order: 'Compensate the tanks!' The chief engineer blew No 8 tank and No 1 opened of its own accord and therefore we blew them all, No 1 as well. No 1 got blown also because it was already open.

Then we went down by the stern. The chief engineer didn't blow the tanks until we were hanging steeply. The commander was standing at an angle on the periscope shaft, the chief engineer was hanging on to the hatch; we were already down by the stern. The chief engineer, in the control room, said, 'I can no longer hold the boat'. The commander ordered, 'Blow the tanks'. It was only a matter of seconds before we should have been done for; the only thing that saved us was that the engines were already running at three-quarter speed. Both engines were put to maximum speed, then came the order, 'All hands into the control room!' I was the last in the forward part of the boat. I was standing there all alone, the others had gone long before. The battery had split, the acid was coming out in a jet, a tongue of flame leapt up in the bow compartment from a fuse box or somewhere. I didn't think that we had any chance when we were down by the stern like that. Not one of us lost his head. When the order 'Open the vents' came, it went like clockwork. They wanted to start up the bilge pump quickly too, but it wouldn't work any longer, because the fuse had been smashed and everything.

We had been attacked by some new kind of depth charge, we could tell from the sound they made, one kind went 'woommmmm' and the others 'woopp'. The things went off, and it was a mystery to us how they could have such an effect. They D/F'd us to the millimetre, with complete accuracy.

And so some of the crew that had hoped to rescue others of their comrades from captivity went into the bag themselves when the escort ships carrying them tied up alongside in Britain. Their conning tower badge, with a steamer half underwater and a wire broom sweeping it away, would be seen no more; their mattress aerial that was fitted when they spent ten days in Danzig would be of no further use.

With the U-boat men now in Britain and out of the war, we return to the Atlantic, to the night when their boat was sunk.

Despite initial favourable conditions the night ended in complete failure for the U-boats which had been kept at a distance and forced to submerge for long periods; so before dawn broke on 20 November U-boat control was making plans for a further attack on the convoy.

A patrol line of *U-714*, *U-843*, *U-424*, *U-212*, *U-391*, *U-967*, *U-538* and *U-542* was ordered for dusk on roughly the 45 degree line. Other U-boats were to form part of the group but to have freedom of movement to the north of the line. Later *U-618* was ordered to join the line to the eastward. Air reconnaissance was to be provided during the day.

Meanwhile, the convoy continued on its way after minor changes of course, although H/F D/F bearings still indicated a number of U-boats ahead of the convoy. *Winchelsea* and *Essington* carried out a sweep on the starboard bow and the 5th Escort Group were stationed at visibility distance on the port bow. At 0940 a Liberator of No 86 Squadron sighted a U-boat through a break in a rain squall about 25 miles on the convoy's port bow. It dived immediately, before an attack could be carried out. *Tweed* and *Lunenburg* were ordered to sweep in the direction, but although they carried out a prolonged search, they found nothing and rejoined the convoy.

Just after midday *Nene* and *Snowberry* were in their day stations eight miles ahead of the port wing column when the latter obtained an asdic contact. *Nene* went to assist and ninety minutes later gained contact. She then carried out two depth charge attacks. After the second attack, two periscope standards were reported and *Nene* increased to full speed. Nothing, however, was sighted and contact could not be regained, and so both ships carried out a search for a further two hours before rejoining the convoy which had altered course at 1600.

In the meantime the Canadian No 422 Squadron, based at Castle Archdale in Northern Ireland, were assisting in escort duties over the convoy. At 1145 G-George W6031 had become airborne. The weather at base was clear and bright as Flying Officer J. D. B. Ulrichson lifted his Sunderland off the water and set course for Donegal Bay en route to the convoy. The pilot was one of three Canadian pilots carried in the eleven-man crew.

Six hours later the Sunderland reported a U-boat sighting. The U-boat was *U-618*, a Type VIIC which had left St Nazaire on its fifth war patrol nine days earlier and was heading to the east of the line as ordered previously. The U-boat was fitted with the new Naxos search receiver and this alerted the gunners of an impending attack; they were ready and shot down the flying boat.

At 1940 an SOS was intercepted in the Azores. This was believed to have come from the Sunderland. An ASR search was carried out from Lagens, but to no avail. Gibraltar and Malta also picked up the SOS but no fix could be obtained.

The U-boat did not immediately report its success to headquarters as there was an order in force to keep W/T silence. At 1300 instructions had been issued that boats were to proceed submerged on a southerly course surfacing at 1900 and bearings were not to be reported until orders were issued. This procedure should have enabled the U-boats to effect a meeting with the convoy although the latter now was on a course which would only just touch the east end of the line.

Control was now expecting the convoy about 1800 and the line was shortened and beacon signals were to be reported immediately. This shortening of the line now made contact less likely especially as the convoy was some way astern of Control's appreciation and was unlikely to meet the U-boats until daybreak. By 1930 before any shadower's bearings had been reported, Control said that no more beacon signals could be expected. At 2240 the line, if not in contact, was to proceed on course until 0500 at 7 knots when they were to remain stationary.

Back to the escorts: At about 1800 H/F D/F activity showed that several U-boats were astern of the convoy. Ninety minutes later *Essington* on the starboard quarter of the extended screen obtained an asdic contact. She then carried out a depth charge attack on the U-boat which was blown to the surface and subsequently disappeared. An underwater explosion was heard and *Winchelsea*, who had been ordered to assist, closed the position and sighted a quantity of oil on the surface.

Then, from H/F D/F bearings and fixes, it appeared that four or five U-boats were moving up from astern to the convoy's port quarter, while two more were approaching the starboard quarter. *Crane*, *Winchelsea* and *Foley* were, therefore, ordered to join the 5th Escort Group, who were then sweeping astern and on the starboard quarter of the convoy.

Just after midnight Escort Group 5 reported that they had twice been illuminated by Leigh lights and starshell which diminished the chances of a surprise attack on the U-boats astern.

The Leigh light aircraft were Liberators of No 53 Squadron. Squadron Leader K. A. Aldrich had taken off from St Eval in N-Nuts, BZ816, at 1530 and nothing more was heard from the aircraft; it had been shot down by the gunners of *U-648*. Wing Commander H. R. A. Edwards, of the same squadron, took off in A-Able nearly eight hours later. B-Baker was also detailed as air escort.

Tweed was sent to investigate a good fix ten miles to the starboard quarter of the convoy while *Crane* and *Foley* were detached to a fix 37 miles on the port beam. Nothing was found.

In the early hours *Pheasant* had obtained a radar contact ahead of the starboard wing column. It faded almost immediately, but was picked up on the asdic two minutes later. An attack was carried out after which contact was lost. All escorts were warned of the possibility of a U-boat having penetrated the outer screen.

The U-boat was *U-969*, which had reported to U-boat headquarters that it was damaged from a depth charge attack. The escorts did not have to worry about it penetrating the screen although it seemed probable that there were at least two U-boats on the port quarter. Liberator A-Able was ordered by the SNO to search out the U-boats and it carried out a depth charge attack sixty miles from the convoy. *Crane* and *Foley*, who were in this area, were ordered to assist. The same aircraft detected another U-boat about fifteen miles on the starboard quarter but owing to the failure of the Leigh light, was unable to carry out an attack. *Watchman* and *Winchelsea* were ordered to hunt for this U-boat but were unable to gain contact.

The U-boat that had been attacked was probably *U-575*, which reported being attacked by an aircraft. Liberator A-Able left the convoy at 0800 and six hours later three engines cut simultaneously while the aircraft was flying at 300 feet. After ditching, the pilot spent ten minutes extracting and inflating the dinghy. None of the other seven members of the crew was visible. The Wing Commander was picked up from the Channel by a trawler at first light the next morning. Like *U-575*, *U-618* and *U-648* also radioed in about being attacked by aircraft and correctly claimed the destruction of their attackers. Other transmissions received at U-boat headquarters reported starshells, hydrophone bearings, Leigh light aircraft, continual radar locations and morse signals, but no sinkings were reported – not even any attacks!

Among U-boats sending in messages during the night had been *U-538*. The previous day it had celebrated one year of life, having been built by the Deutsche Werft Hamburg. Its commander was Kapitänleutnant Johann-Egbert Gossler. It left Kiel on its first patrol on 2 October and had been in the Atlantic area between the Azores and Spain before joining the pack at line 3, and had no successes to report.

At 0420 *Foley* had obtained a radar contact, about forty miles on the convoy's port quarter. Shortly afterwards *Crane* also picked it up and on illuminating sighted *U-538*, describing the Type IXC$_{40}$ as 'a large U-boat', on the surface. When the range had closed to about 500 yards the U-boat dived. *Crane* dropped one 'scare' charge and then carried out a deliberate attack. *Foley*, whose asdic was out of action, was ordered to carry out a radar search round the position. After a time *Crane* attacked again and four minutes later heard an explosion astern which was presumed to be a gnat. The ship's speed at this time was 8 knots. A creeping attack was then carried out by *Foley*, at 0600, with *Crane* as directing ship, but it was not very accurate. Forty minutes later *Crane* fired her last ten-charge pattern and had only six depth charges remaining.

Now began a prolonged chase in which the U-boat ejected many SBT's and used every trick its commander knew, but the tenacious sloop hung on and never lost contact. Finally, at 1005, she was able to direct *Foley* in a creeping attack in which eighteen charges were dropped. After the attack by the frigate no firm contact could be re-established. On investigation a distinct patch of oil was sighted. *Winchelsea* and *Watchman* joined about this time and reported that they had found some wreckage. Just after midday *Crane* and *Foley* shaped course to rejoin, leaving the two destroyers to continue the search for souvenirs. They remained in the area for a further two hours, during which time *Watchman* carried out a hedgehog and three depth charge attacks. These were probably on oil and wreckage from *U-538*, which had already sunk, taking all its crew with it.

Meanwhile, at dawn, the 5th and 7th Groups had carried out line abreast searches on the port and starboard quarters respectively and combined for the sweep back to the convoy.

At this same time, in France at U-boat headquarters they seemed to have realised that the third and final night's effort had been a failure; the line was ordered to dive and move off to the southward and U-boats were told, rather plaintively, not to forget their gnats. At midday the operation was officially ended and the usual post-mortem report was issued. U-boats were told that they had engaged in a hard fight with an enemy who had collected together a particularly strong defence. The lack of success was due partly to this strong defence and partly to the scanty air reconnaissance on the decisive day. The report continued: 'The fight goes on. Strongest air reconnaissance on the decisive day, closest concentration of boats in place and time – that is attack in one night only – are to shape the conditions on which will depend the success which your old fighting spirit must achieve.'

Clearly the whole operation was planned with hope of considerable ' success which, if achieved, would have materially affected the spirit of the crews and their ability to renew the Atlantic battle. Operations in the North Atlantic had been fruitless for a long time and it was hoped to boost morale with a concentrated attack during three successive nights by three separate attacking lines with the addition of three homeward-bound boats.

It had not been possible to make use of evasive routing for the convoys and they actually followed a route quite favourable to the U-boats. There was little doubt that the policy of relying solely on night attacks and then directing these attacks in the first place at escort ships resulted in defeat largely because of the vigilance of the sea and air escorts.

Part of the summing up from U-boat headquarters read:

The second, and particularly the third, night of the attack showed that in this area the Allies, having once located the U-boats, are able to engage them speedily and effectively with numerous night-flying aircraft and strong surface escort forces. . . . The next operation in this area must therefore be planned for one night only, the disposition being as close as possible, so that a large number of boats may be concentrated round the convoy . . .

Of lessons to be learned from the attack it was observed:

The operation again demonstrated the impossibility of conducting proper reconnaissance and U-boat direction with only a handful of aircraft. The convoy's position had to be established not once or twice in 24 hours, but every four hours at least, otherwise it was impossible to manoeuvre the submerged U-boats ahead of the convoy in time, or to counter a diversionary change of course. While it was gratifying to confirm that aircraft were able, with their radar, to maintain contact with a convoy at night, it was unfortunate that beacon signals alone did not indicate the convoy position with sufficient accuracy for the U-boats, which at night had to rely exclusively on visual sighting. A visual aid was needed, such as a marker-bomb, which could be recognised by the U-boats but could not be imitated; moreover, a signal of this kind was the only means of countering diversionary starshell fire. The U-boats' successes against enemy aircraft were remarkable. On the last night quite a number of attacks were repelled and two aircraft were shot down, with one or two sending out distress signals on their return flight.

The reasons for the poor results against the ships of the convoy were obvious. The U-boats had been seriously impeded in air and sea escorts of unprecedented strength and, in the nocturnal mêlée, had failed to gain bearing through having to take avoiding action against air and surface radar, diving because of the approach of aircraft or destroyers and fighting off aircraft. The convoy's outer screen had been reinforced by units of the hunter groups operating in the western part of the Bay of Biscay, and none managed to force it, despite the use of the T5 torpedo, which had, however, failed to come up to expectation.

While other escort groups had been heavily occupied attacking U-boats HM ships *Bentinck*, *Byard*, *Calder*, *Bazely* and *Drury*, all new Captain class frigates, had been at their base at Pollock Dock Belfast. These purpose-built U-boat attackers, of just under 2,000 tons, had quickly made their mark in the Battle of the Atlantic. Together they made up the 4th Escort Group and in the late forenoon on 19 November they sailed from Belfast and swept down the Irish Sea at 18 knots to cover initially the homeward bound convoy.

A day out at sea, in a position 60 miles south-west of the Fastnet Rock, an asdic contact was made, but despite a four-hour search and six depth charge attacks nothing substantial could be reported.

In darkness, eleven hours later, *Bentinck* heard a close U-boat transmission in the direction of the convoy but no attack was made.

Early the next afternoon the escort group closed the convoy and then proceeded as previously ordered by the Commander-in-Chief Western Atlantic to operate independently. They had just about reached their pre-planned positions when the Germans attacked with glider bombs.

We will leave the convoy for a moment to mention the Luftwaffe in the context of the convoys in the Atlantic. First it must be said that Hermann Goering, chief of the Luftwaffe, was always against using his aircraft in support of U-boats and was often at odds with Admiral Dönitz and his predecessor Admiral Raeder. However, there was a Luftwaffe station at Bordeaux-Merignac where its leader was known as Fliegerführer Atlantik. Amongst other squadrons, there was Heavy Bomber Unit 40, Kampfgeschwader 40, or KG40.

At the end of October 1943 the unit received a detachment of He177 aircraft. This four motor bomber had the appearance of a twin-engined aircraft as its two engine nacelles each enclosed a pair of DB601 liquid-cooled in-line engines driving a single four-blade propeller. As mentioned earlier German aircraft had already attempted to work with the U-boat packs attacking convoy MKS30/SL139 and on the 20th two of these shadowers had been shot down, one in the morning and the other in the evening, off Cape Ortegal by Beaufighters operating from Gibraltar. The next day it was hoped that the He177's would exact revenge on their first operation from the French base. Twenty-five aircraft, each carrying a Hs293 glider bomb, were scrambled; the convoy was 800 miles from their base. The glider bomb which had a wingspan of ten feet and carried a 1,100lb warhead was controlled by the navigator in the He177. The missile was guided towards its target at 370mph by radio signals.

At about 1530 the aircraft started attacking the convoy with their glider bombs and the escorts were ordered to 'pack'. While the attack was at its height the convoy's anti-aircraft ship joined and was ordered to zig-zag across the stern of the convoy. *Marsa*, of 4,405 tons, straggled about three-and-a-half miles astern and was repeatedly attacked until finally hit and had to be abandoned. A little later *Delius* was damaged and set on fire, but eventually managed to reach harbour. The crew of *Marsa* were picked up by *Petunia* and *Essington*, but some of the officers were transferred to *Delius* as she had lost all but one of her deck officers. After 90 minutes the attack ended and the enemy aircraft withdrew. In all about sixteen bombs were dropped, only two found their mark. This was considered to be due to the heavy anti-aircraft fire put up by the escort which appeared to deter the attackers.

Two aircraft failed to return but the attack was considered as a success by the Germans as two large ships were claimed as sunk and three others damaged. The attack revealed possibilities of practical co-operation between aircraft and U-boats in convoy attacks. Although there was little prospect of this in the subsequent months because of the limited range of the He177, U-boat headquarters hoped that the first successful attempt would inspire the Luftwaffe to further operations of the same nature; but this was not to be, for the He177s were transferred shortly afterwards to the Mediterranean.

Back at sea the rest of the day passed without incident, and at dawn the next day *Winchelsea* and *Watchman* were detached-as their fuel situation was becoming critical. The former had also received some damage by a 'near-miss' aircraft attack.

Just before noon on 23rd *Essington* and *Foley* left as ordered and at 1700 the convoy was split into fast and slow sections; both parts finally reached the United Kingdom without further incident. The LST's made their own way.

As there seemed to be no sign of any U-boats the escorts from the convoy dispersed. The Fourth Escort Group turned to the westward in the morning of 22 November in the direction of the southbound convoy OS59.

The Luftwaffe was also seeking the convoy at this time, but without success.

Meanwhile, after three hours, the Fourth Escort Group were joined by *Blackwood*, another Captain class frigate, that had sailed late. The Group then split into two, *Bentinck*, *Byard* and *Calder* in the first division and *Blackwood*, *Bazely* and *Drury* in the second.

In the meantime the fourteen U-boats still on patrol after the unsuccessful interceptions were ordered south-westward at high speed. During this movement enemy 'destroyers' were sighted. These were presumably the Captain class frigates. The Germans correctly assumed they were a hunter group.

An hour before midnight, when the second division was stationed ten miles astern of the first, *Blackwood* obtained a radar contact at a range of over five miles. The first division continued towards the convoy while *Blackwood* and the second division took over the hunt.

The U-boat was almost certainly *U-648*, which had shot down the No 53 Squadron Liberator two nights previously. The Hamburg-built boat constructed at the Blohm and Voss yard had been launched fourteen months earlier under the command of Oberleutnant Peter Stahl. On its first cruise, from Kiel, it shot down a training aircraft from No 10 Squadron. This patrol, which began on 3 April, ended on 19 May when the crew were pleased to put into Brest, thus escaping the Atlantic holocaust which accounted for so many of their colleagues during the month. The Type VIIC boat was ordered to the Caribbean area and sailed on 1 July but because of the sinking of the mid-Atlantic refuelling U-boats *U-648* became a reserve fueller and returned to St Nazaire on 10 August. Two months later it left the Biscay base and joined up with other U-boats searching for convoys.

U-boat headquarters had been receiving reports of sightings of destroyers and it was correctly assessed that these were hunter groups. Among those reporting in was *U-648*, a U-boat that had achieved more successes against aircraft than ships.

As *Blackwood* closed the position shown up on the radar screen the U-boat dived. Picking up asdic contact the frigate carried out a depth charge attack and *Drury* carried out two further attacks. After these attacks contact was lost.

A thorough search of the area was made until just after 0600 when *Bazely* obtained a radar contact. Six minutes later she illuminated a U-boat which dived. Asdic contact was obtained and an attack made. Then *Bazely* detected, by radar, a U-boat, probably the same one, at five miles' range, it dived when the range had closed to 4,000 yards. Asdic contact was quickly gained and thereafter a series of attacks was carried out. In all *Drury* made eight depth charge attacks, *Blackwood* six attacks and *Bazely* seven depth charge and one hedgehog attacks. Two of *Blackwood*'s attacks were 'creepers', one being directed by *Drury* and the other by *Bazely*. Because it had been found that some of *Blackwood*'s depth charges had been firing shallower than the set depth it was not considered prudent to attack at 5 knots, but the higher speed robbed this type of attack of its principal advantage, the undetected approach of the attacking vessel to the U-boat. In each case only twelve charges were fired instead of the prescribed 26 and it was, therefore, unlikely that the area of the pattern covered the errors to be expected in this form of attack.

The attack was finally abandoned just before midday. Errors or not, *U-648* had been sunk, although at the time this was not realised, and was only credited to the second division later; hence my writing earlier that the U-boat was 'almost certainly' *U-648* which had been attacked at about midnight and six hours later. No other U-boat signalled in about being attacked at these times, so I think my conclusion is correct and that the boat was sunk during the morning watch on 23 November.

In the report of the attacks by *Blackwood* the ship's company are blamed: 'It is considered that the failure of the depth charges to fire at the set depth was probably due to bad drill.'

There were anti-U-boat sweeps for the rest of 23rd and all the next day, during which time the first division had met convoy OS59, satisfied itself that the 39th Escort Group were giving it adequate protection before putting into Horta, in the Azores, to refuel.

After unsuccessfully searching for 36 hours the second division were rewarded with two firm contacts within twenty minutes in the small hours of 25 November.

First, *Drury* picked up a radar contact at seven-and-a-half miles and while she was giving chase *Bazely* picked up another contact. *Blackwood* joined *Bazely* in the hunt for this nearer U-boat, *U-600*.

The U-boat, together with the others who had been unsuccessfully seeking southbound convoys OS59 and KMS30, had been switched to search for a big northbound convoy SL140/MKS31 but unfortunately ran into the Second Division of the 4th Escort Group about 210 miles north of the Azores.

U-600 was a most successful Type VIIC boat, of the 3rd Flotilla, launched over two years earlier and like *U-648* was from the Blohm and Voss yard at Hamburg and under the command of Kapitänleutnant Bernhard zur Mühlen.

Nine months elapsed between *U-600*'s launch and its first war cruise, out of Kiel, on 14 July 1942. The cruise was to the Gulf of Mexico and was blessed with success. On 10 August a small British sailing vessel was gunned and sunk in the Caribbean. Three days later *U-600* intercepted convoy TAW12 from Trinidad to the United States and sank a 4,520 ton Latvian ship *Everelza* which exploded in a column of fire over 200 yards high as its cargo of fuel erupted. The commodore's ship, the 5,000 ton American *Delmundo*, sank five minutes after being hit with a stern torpedo. The U-boat experienced some of its own medicine when returning to base at La Pallice, for off the Gironde estuary it triggered off a submarine laid mine and was damaged but arrived back in port the next day, 22 September.

It was two months before *U-600* was back at sea, on a North Atlantic patrol. This time its only recorded success was the 6,762 ton American ship *James McKay*, torpedoed and sunk on 8 December. The U-boat arrived back on 27 December, in time to see in 1943. After leave the crew were back again on 11 February for what was to be their most successful patrol, again to the North Atlantic.

Thirteen days out, with *U-628*, attacking convoy ON166 it sank the Norwegian 4,391 ton ship *Ingria*. It was during March when U-boat headquarters were reading British signals that U-boats were so positioned to intercept convoys. Three times *U-600* was in contact with HX229 and before dawn on 17 March four FAT's were fired, then the U-boat turned away and fired from the stern tubes. In quick succession three ships were brought to a halt. The British 8,714 ton ship *Nariva* was hit by one torpedo, the American 6,125 ton *Irenee du Pont* was hit by two torpedoes and *Southern Princess* the British whaling depot ship was hit by a fourth torpedo. A rescue ship picked up 138 survivors from the American ship and the whaling ship by dawn. Four boatloads of survivors from *Nariva* were picked up by an escort ship, HMS *Anemone*. *Southern Princess*, which had been burning fiercely up to the bridge, capsized and overturned floating for half-an-hour before sinking at 1000. The American ship was given the *coup de grâce* by *U-91* in the afternoon, but *Nariva* was reboarded and eventually arrived at Liverpool, badly damaged. An elated U-boat crew returned to La Pallice on 26 March.

The next patrol, which commenced on 25 April, was cut short when the boat collided with *U-407* west of Spain; both were damaged and *U-600* arrived back at base on 11 May. A month later *U-600* was on patrol again, this time to the West African coast, for in the meantime Admiral Dönitz had temporarily withdrawn U-boats from the Battle of the Atlantic following the loss of the 41 boats in May. On this patrol *U-600* was slightly damaged by an air attack, but shot down its attacker. This three month cruise was its longest and the U-boat did not put to sea again for two months, this time from Brest where it had returned to after the aircraft damage.

The sixth and last patrol of *U-600* was to the Spain-Azores area and began on 7 November; the U-boat was one of the pack forming the southernmost line to intercept the northbound combined convoy SL139/MKS30, as already recounted.

Seeing the two frigates approaching *U-600* dived and apparently went deep immediately. Asdic contact was made and 24 minutes later, *Bazely* which had only one depth charge pattern remaining, carried out four hedgehog attacks. The last, just after 0300, was successful; 28 seconds after firing, a heavy explosion shook the ships. After this attack both *Bazely* and *Blackwood* maintained contact and the latter dropped a ten-charge pattern after four minutes had elapsed. Contact finally faded in both ships; *U-600* and all its crew had perished.

Bazely remained to watch for wreckage in accordance with instructions:

Recognition of concrete evidence confirming destruction of a submerged U-boat, is of the greatest value, first for purposes of Admiralty planning and secondly to ensure that the attacker does not waste time when he is better employed elsewhere. There is, too, the equally strong incentive – tangible proof of achievement.

Oil will certainly and air bubbles almost certainly appear on the surface eventually; they will not as a rule be seen at night or in rough weather, unless appearing in great quantities and continuously. In any case, unless they do so appear, they are not proof positive.

The rise for solids depends on a number of factors – specific gravity of the object, depth at which detached, impetus up or down due to pressure wave of explosion and temporary imprisonment in the hull of the U-boat.

Blackwood had meanwhile joined *Drury* who had been unsuccessful in her attacks on the other U-boat. *Bazely* joined in the afternoon and was ordered to sweep five miles outside the other two ships. As no contact had been obtained by 1630, course was set in order to join the first division, which was met twenty minutes later, having sailed from Horta the previous evening.

Shortly afterwards orders were received for the group to support convoy SL140/MKS31 to the south-eastward.

Owing to the considerable swell which had now got up it was found impossible to transfer depth charges to the second division. It was therefore detached at 2230. *Bazely* and *Drury* proceeding in company and *Blackwood* following at 16 knots, having one engine out of action.

In the early hours of 26th, as the result of sighting tracer fired by a U-boat at an aircraft, *Bazely* obtained a radar contact on the bearing and gave chase with *Drury* in company. The U-boat dived and, on reaching the position, both ships commenced searching; *Drury* obtained asdic contact and carried out a hedgehog attack. She then dropped her four remaining depth charges and fired a second hedgehog salvo before finally losing contact. The U-boat being attacked was *U-618*, which it will be recalled had shot down a Sunderland a few days earlier. Now its firing at another aircraft had given its position away to the hunting group.

The first division joined at 0315 and took over the search from *Bazely* and *Drury* who then resumed course for Horta.

Bentinck obtained asdic contact with the U-boat and for the next seven hours contacts were attacked by all ships. During these attacks ten depth charge patterns and seven hedgehog salvoes were fired but no results were achieved. Contact was finally lost in the late morning; Kapitänleutnant Kurt Baberg had shown as much skill underwater as his gunners had on the surface, *U-618* had escaped but was badly damaged.

The Fourth Escort Group then joined the convoy and its escorts.

The convoy of 68 merchantmen had been proceeding towards the British Isles escorted by Group B1 with HM ships *Hurricane, Glenarm, Dahlia, Borage, Meadowsweet, Honeysuckle, Oxlip* and *Wanderer*. In the afternoon the Second Escort Group, consisting of *Starling, Wild Goose, Kite* and *Magpie* joined; Captain Walker was Captain (D) of the group and as senior officer took control of the escorts comprising sixteen in number.

Various contacts were made by the hunting groups during the day and there were a considerable number of unexplained explosions. These were probably acoustic, or ordinary, torpedoes exploding at the end of their runs.

The Luftwaffe had sighted the convoy steering a westerly course and the U-boat pack was moved accordingly, but as soon as the shadowing aircraft had headed back to base the convoy altered course to the north, and when sighted from the air again the next morning it was to the eastwards of the U-boats. The boats then proceeded submerged to the north-east, surfacing in the evening to take up pursuit at high speed.

After dark a BV222 shadowed the convoy. However, although its homing signals were picked up, the bearings were too acute for an accurate fix. Weather conditions were favourable, but the U-boats made little headway.

Once the U-boats had broken surface a flock of H/F D/F transmissions were picked up to the westwards of the escort and support groups. *Hurricane*, senior officer's ship of B1, received or transmitted over 300 signals that night alone, and the ship, together with *Bentinck* and *Blackwood*, gave chase. Many U-boats were misled and delayed in reaching the convoy by starshell used by the groups to create a diversion. This was a speciality of escorts under the command of Captain Walker.

It will be remembered that F-Freddie of 179 Squadron had sunk *U-211* earlier. The 179 Squadron detachment at Lagens was in the nature of a stop-gap pending the arrival of the full No 172 Squadron. On the evening of 27 November two Wellington XIV's were rostered for convoy escort duty, the first, O-Orange HF153, was captained by Pilot Officer T. B. Wilkin, an experienced squadron pilot. The other aircraft, L-Lucy HF168, was flown by

HMS *Starling* (*Inset* Captain F. J. Walker)

HMS *Magpie*

Squadron Leader R. G. Knott and his crew from the 179 Squadron detachment. The latter crew boarded their aircraft and were airborne from Lagens just before 2000. Because it was dark they did not see the dust kicked up by their take-off. Their object was an air escort above the convoy.

L-Lucy was over 400 miles from base, to the north-east of Madeira, when the convoy was reached just before midnight. The wireless operator picked up some ship to ship R/T but as his sensitive fingers slowly twisted the dial no ship to aircraft signal was picked up; the pilot thus carried out a routine anti-U-boat search at a distance of fifteen miles round the convoy. An hour into this boring procedure, while flying at 700 feet an ASV contact was made at four miles, to port. The contact was a U-boat, *U-542*.

The U-boat was a large, Type IXC$_{40}$ boat under the command of Oberleutnant Christian-Brandt Coester. Constructed at the Deutsche Werft in Hamburg just ten months earlier, it was on its first patrol. It had left Kiel on 2 October for the Azores-Spain area of the Atlantic. It will be remembered that *U-542* was one of the pack waiting on the 45 degree line for the convoy. Earlier, on 16 November, the commander had signalled to U-boat headquarters that he had attacked an escort ship, but without success; after seven minutes a torpedo was heard to explode at the end of its run.

As the Wellington homed in, it saw the U-boat too soon to permit the use of the Leigh light. The aircraft continued on course, and at five miles regained contact. This time the Leigh light was switched on at half-mile range, while the pilot thought he was flying at 300 feet. Owing to a defect, no marine altimeter was fitted and when the U-boat was illuminated the pilot could see that he was flying at approximately 600 feet, much too high for a successful attack; he therefore continued on course passing over the target and turned again, rapidly losing height. The light was again switched on at half-a-mile; this time an attack was carried out with six depth charges straddling *U-542* at right angles to track. Three depth charges were estimated to overshoot to starboard, two were believed to have exploded on impact and the last overshot to port, the stick falling just abaft the conning tower. During the attack the Wellington's front gunner opened fire and the Germans responded with light flak. The U-boat remained stationary on the surface throughout the

HMS *Wild Goose*: HM Queen Elizabeth talks with the officers . . .

. . . while HM King George VI inspects the men

attack. The pilot thought that the U-boat had already been disabled and was unable to submerge before his attack. After the attack *U-542* still remained on the surface but there was no further fire from its guns.

The SOE was informed of the attack and the U-boat's position, and a sea marker was dropped as the Wellington had reached the prudent limit of its endurance and fuel was running low. The aircraft's wireless operator received no response to his R/T signals but he knew his message had been received as he heard it being repeated from ship to ship, giving the U-boat's position. The Wellington then left the scene and made for the nearest landfall, which happened to be Gibraltar, and touched down at the Rock at dawn.

When the crew were debriefed they were asked if they had seen any sign of O-Orange, which had so far failed to return. At 2015 an SOS was picked up from the Wellington at land bases, but had not been received by L-Lucy, which had been having trouble with its receiver, and at this time had not long been airborne from the Azores.

As there were no survivors from the Wellington, or from *U-542*, it will never be known exactly what happened. At 2022 *Starling* and *Kite* sighted a searchlight beam and heard a ripple of firing. At this time it was thought to be an encounter by a United States task force, but the beam was probably from O-Orange as previously the ships had picked up a message from the Wellington reporting the sighting of a U-boat at 2013.

Perhaps it is not unreasonable to assume that O-Orange attacked and disabled *U-542* and was then shot down, hence the SOS. Squadron Leader Knott had reported that he thought the U-boat had been previously disabled and unable to submerge. It seems that Pilot Officer Wilkin and his crew were unlucky; Oberleutnant Coester and his crew were lucky with the first Wellington, but unlucky that a second aircraft came along when they were unable to submerge and vulnerable, and that Squadron Leader Knott was extremely fortunate when *U-542* obliged by staying on the surface while he was making height adjustments for his attack.

The end of *U-542* will never be known for certain; it probably sank soon after the second aircraft's attack. After L-Lucy had

Depth charge attack from HMS *Exe*

transmitted the position of the attack and returned to base *Starling* was ordered to close the position indicated by the sea marker. While on the way to this position she was ordered to alter course to go to the assistance of *Wild Goose*.

About ten miles on the port bow of the convoy *Wild Goose* had obtained a radar contact and sighted a U-boat in the light of starshell before forcing it to dive. Asdic contact was picked up but was very soon lost, and it appeared that the U-boat had gone deep. An explosion was heard, which may have been a gnat exploding at the end of its run. A search was then carried out with *Magpie*, but it was not until after 0100 that asdic contact was again established, probably with the same U-boat. *Wild Goose* trailed it until *Starling*'s arrival about an hour later. The U-boat surfaced at 0246, was immediately detected by radar and promptly dived as both ships opened fire. For the next two-and-half hours attacks were carried out, including one creeping attack by *Wild Goose*, but no results were observed. In view of the possibility of an air attack on the convoy, the sloops then left the area to rejoin. The U-boat attacked was almost certainly *U-764*, whose commander, Oberleutnant Hanskurt von Bremen, reported firing a gnat and hearing an end of run detonation after fourteen minutes.

There was intense U-boat activity during the remainder of the night from the fifteen boats within striking range, but the main threat had come just before dawn – and from a rare type of U-boat.

The U-boat was *U-107*, a Type IXB of which only fourteen were built and only three others still remained afloat. The U-boat, launched way back in the summer of 1940, was under the command of Kapitänleutnant Volker Simmermacher.

The attack by *U-107* was to be the last one during the night. At 0622 the Flower Class corvette *Dahlia*, on the starboard beam, obtained a radar contact between herself and the convoy. Owing to the size of the echo, it was thought that this might be an escort out of station. Indeed, the U-boat had an overall length of 251 feet and the lengths of the varying size of the escorts ranged between 200 and 290 feet. Had the U-boat commander kept his nerve and remained on the surface he might have got away with it, but when the radar echo failed after three minutes and an asdic contact was picked up, there could be no doubt that it was a U-boat, and what was more it had penetrated the close screen in a preliminary manoeuvre similar to that carried out by Kretschmer and the other Atlantic aces in the earlier days. Eight minutes after *U-107* had dived *Dahlia* heard two explosions, separated by a few seconds, which were thought to be torpedo explosions at the end of their run. Simmermacher reported one end of run gnat explosion from the torpedo aimed at the escort.

An accurate attack was carried out on *U-107*, the only one of the pack with sufficient determination to penetrate the inner screen, and considerable damage was caused to the Type IXB boat, but it reached harbour. Except on this occasion, all the other U-boats had dived at some distance from the screen.

When *Dahlia* swept back through the position it was reported from aft that the water was covered with oil. She continued searching the area until after dawn, when course was set to rejoin on the arrival of *Bentinck*. The latter attempted to recover samples of oil with little success. On rejoining the convoy she reported that bubbles of oil were still coming to the surface an hour-and-a-half after the attack.

After this climax to the battle no more close transmissions were

D/F'd and no more U-boat contacts were obtained. At daylight the convoy's course was altered twenty degrees to starboard until it was fifteen miles off track so as to upset any U-boats which might be taking up positions for a submerged daylight attack. The U-boats had, however, evidently given up the struggle, as aircraft patrols produced no sighting reports. The support groups remained in the vicinity during the day to give anti-aircraft protection in the event of an air attack. After dark several long signals were D/F'd well astern of the convoy and after this nothing more was heard from the pack of U-boats.

The convoy proceeded without further incident and, after being hove to and scattered for one night, finally reached the United Kingdom, unscathed, on 5 December.

CHAPTER FIVE

American Aircraft Carriers

Ascension Island, a British possession, is situated in the South Atlantic midway between Africa and South America. In November 1942 the American strategic zone was enlarged to include the volcanic island in the operation of their VLR aircraft; Ascension made possible the effectuation of a barrier to prevent surfaced U-boats en route to the southern hemisphere areas from passing undetected through the South Atlantic narrows between the bulge of Brazil and West Africa.

A year later the USN VB-107 Bombing Squadron had accounted for *U-598* in July and helped in the sinking of *U-604* the following month.

Now, in the last week of the month they were seeking a southbound U-boat which had been sighted by an aircraft from USS *Memphis* on 17 November. Although they did not know it at the time, the boat was a U-cruiser, *U-849*, a Type IXD$_2$ which had left Kiel for the Indian Ocean on 2 October. The boat had been launched from the A. G. Weser yard at Bremen a year earlier and Kapitänleutnant Heinz-Otto Schultze was appointed in command.

The commander had, in the past fifteen months, built himself a reputation; as commander of *U-432* he had sunk fifteen ships totalling over 50,000 tons, earning himself a Knight's Cross. His sinkings included a 42 ton boat and a steamer of nearly 10,000 tons, they all came alike to him and each one was sunk with torpedo or gunfire. He carried out Dönitz's basic principle: 'Better a few ships destroyed than many damaged.'

The new commander was upset, in March 1943, to hear that his old boat had been sunk in the Atlantic, but he quickly put this behind him and threw himself into the task of getting the crew of *U-849* to peak efficiency. Perhaps, in the light of future events, the one thing that was not emphasised strongly enough from the handbook for U-boat commanders was the paragraph on the importance of keeping a good look-out:

> In every situation, whether under way or in the course of attacking, the saying is true of the U-boat, 'He who sights first has won'. An untiring, alert look-out is responsible for the success and safety of the U-boat, and thus constitutes a means both of offensive and defensive. Owing to its high speed the aircraft is the most dangerous enemy of the U-boat. For this reason, by day and on moonlight nights, the sky must be watched with particular care.

Before leaving Kiel *U-849* was fitted with the Naxos, a radar set just being introduced into service. It had a separate aerial that had to be brought down the conning tower hatch for diving.

All was going well when the boat radioed U-boat headquarters on 6 November. Eleven days later it was seen by the aircraft from USS *Memphis* and the USN air force base at Ascension was put on alert as the U-boat was heading their way. Persistent long range sweeps followed the sighting and at first light on 25 November two Liberators took off on an anti-U-boat patrol. Owing to wireless difficulties the aircraft lost touch with each other, but one pilot, Lieutenant M. Vance Dawkins of the USN Reserve, takes up the story of what happened as he was flying above broken stratus clouds covering from 2-4,000 feet in his aircraft camouflaged with white painted undersides and blue-grey topsides, four hours into his patrol:

> At 0645 I departed from Ascension Island on an anti-U-boat sweep. The squadron for the past two days had been operating on a new frequency and I experienced difficulty contacting 107-8 which was participating in the sweep. The last communication I had with him prior to the attack was at 1000 and that was weak.
> While flying at 5,200 feet my co-pilot sighted a target about thirty degrees off the starboard bow which was readily identified

as a U-boat by myself and the navigator. The range was about ten miles. I sounded the warning horn and gave instructions to the navigator to check the intervolometer and the U-boat's position. The photographer was ordered to man his station. The original altitude was maintained while course was changed. At about five miles' range I ordered an 'SSS' signal sent. I began a rapid descent through clouds and broke through at 2,000 feet, one mile astern of the target. I attacked the U-boat, releasing bombs while in a steep glide, with an intervalometer spacing of sixty feet at 200 mph. My target angle was about 160 degrees and altitude 25 feet. Six bombs were released which were observed to envelop the U-boat in one large detonation, two bombs falling close to the starboard quarter, three close to the port beam – while the sixth possibly struck the U-boat's deck. After the drop my tail turret strafed the conning tower and deck on which a few personnel were seen. The crown turret and nose guns did not fire due to the suddenness of the attack. Chow was being served at the time of sighting which led to some confusion aboard.

I thought it advisable not to delay the attack until these guns were ready as the element of surprise might be lost. As it was the U-boat was taken completely off guard and not a shot was fired until after we passed over the conning tower.

As the plane cleared the conning tower, I felt a loss of control in the rudders while the nose dropped badly. I lost further altitude and nearly struck the water, but I pulled heavily back on the yoke and the plane climbed slowly to 800 feet where I observed ack-ack fire short and below the plane. The U-boat gave out a large oil slick and had no way on it. It had been blown 45 degrees to port. I ordered the navigator to prepare the three remaining bombs for the drop and the co-pilot to contact 107-8 and advise of an attack and position for him to home on me. I climbed up to 1,500 feet and out of range of the ack-ack fire. The other aircraft could not be contacted but base picked up the message and relayed it. Observing that the U-boat was severely crippled and not knowing the extent of damage to my plane, I did not think it advisable to deliver a second attack until 107-8 arrived. However, I kept the plane within striking distance and ordered all hands to observe closely any attempt of the U-boat to submerge. While circling the

U-849 under attack

U-boat I was informed by the after station and the bow that the crew was abandoning the U-boat. I closed in on the target rapidly to take pictures but while one mile from the U-boat, it exploded some 200 feet in the air. Thereafter I dropped to about 500 feet and took pictures of survivors. I finally contacted 107-8 at 1125 and advised him of the attack and sinking. Five minutes later I departed the area.

The Station Commander commented:

It was remarkable that the sighting was at a range of ten miles despite the fact that radar, in good working condition was in use and that the U-boat was fully surfaced. The obvioius conclusion is that the plane's radar was not directed at the U-boat at any time. It follows also that the U-boat was not using radar.

The attack was excellent in all respects. The pilot retained his advantage of surprise by skilful use of cloud cover and by the swiftness with which he prepared and delivered his attack. The drop was extremely accurate and deadly. Photographs of the drop were taken from a camera mount in the tunnel hatch. Pictures of survivors in the water were taken from the waist hatch at such an altitude that it was difficult to detect them. However, study reveals them quite clearly, scattered through the oil slick.

The voice radio transmissions were received at the base, 550 miles distant. That they were not received by 107-8, about thirty miles distant was doubtless the fault of a defective radio receiver. Consequently 107-8 did not receive a contact report until 1115 when it was relayed from the base. Thereafter it attempted to join the attacking plane at the scene of the action. No communications were established between planes until the distance was closed to less than twenty miles. The second plane then made a short unsuccessful search for survivors and followed the damaged plane home, standing by to render assistance if it became necessary.

The damage incurred by the attacker was from fragments of a depth charge which apparently broke up on striking the water. One such fragment of the flat nose, torn across the diameter through the fuse hole and just aft of the weld along the circumference, lodged in the centre leading edge of the starboard vertical stabilizer of the plane. In addition there were small scratches and tears in the fabric of the plane.

Photographs show some twenty Germans in the water. A liferaft was dropped but no survivors were rescued. Kapitänleutnant Heinz-Otto Schultze, who in *U-432* had carried out many pack attacks, had been lost in his new boat before he could get to the rich pickings expected against independently routed ships in the Indian Ocean.

The next boat off the Bremen slip, *U-850*, launched five weeks after *U-849*, was following and its story will be taken up shortly. It was the victim of a US carrier-borne aircraft.

Unlike their four-engined colleagues on Ascension, who once they had landed could relax and get a good night's sleep knowing there was no chance of their being attacked, the single-engined aircraft pilots on the carriers were always at risk of being torpedoed.

At an Atlantic convoy conference held in Washington at the beginning of March 1943 it was agreed that the United States Navy would protect the southern route through the Atlantic henceforth. This naval force, a support hunter group, sometimes called a task force, would comprise an escort carrier and five destroyers, under British control.

The aircraft that the various carriers would fly were Avengers and Martlets, built by the Grumman corporation. It was due to the foresight of the manufacturers, back in 1935, with their basic aircraft technologies and the availability of air-cooled radial engines, variable pitch propellers, metal structure techniques and efficient aerodynamic configurations, that carried the navy aircraft design through the war.

The F4F-3, Martlet, in correct flying balance, controllable and with a few minor exceptions was found to be satisfactory for use in taking off from and landing on a carrier.

In 1938, with the war clouds gathering in Europe, British and French purchasing commissions visited the United States looking for aircraft. The French became interested in the Martlet as a carrier fighter and one hundred were ordered in the autumn of 1939. By this time, at the beginning of the war, President Roosevelt declared a 'limited national emergency'. In May 1940 Congress authorised

Grumman Avengers

the US Navy to increase its inventory by 15,000 aircraft.

With the fall of France in June Britain assumed delivery of the French Martlets, and from this time Martlet became the official name of the F4F, although they later became known as Wildcats. The Martlet was the first aircraft to enter service equipped with an engine having a two-stage supercharger.

In September 1941 Martlets, flying from HMS *Audacity*, shot down a FW200 Condor, the first of a number of such aircraft to fall to the fighter's guns.

The ubiquitous Avenger, TBF-1, performed as a day and night bomber, dive bomber and torpedo bomber, carrying a 2,000lb load of bombs, torpedoes or, more usually, depth charges. This loading caused it to be underpowered but the chunky aircraft played a vital part in attacking single U-boats and wolf packs in the Atlantic.

The first of the US Atlantic carriers was USS *Bogue*, which had been converted to a carrier from a mercantile hull. The carrier was 520 feet long and carried twelve Wildcat and nine Avenger aircraft.

Aircraft from *Bogue* sank four Atlantic U-boats in a two month period from the end of May in a convoy support role and now, at the end of November and on its eighth cruise, the carrier was ordered to carry out a new, strictly offensive, mission. Freed from convoy escort duties *Bogue* left America on 14 November bound for an area where U-boats were known to be working and now carried twelve Avengers and nine Wildcats.

The first victim was *U-86* on 29 November. The Type VIIC boat had done remarkably well, surviving for two years in the Atlantic while carrying out eight war patrols. A graduate of the 1934 class, Kapitänleutnant Walter Schug commissioned the boat when it was launched from the Flenderwerft at Lübeck on 10 May 1941. Its first war cruise commenced from Kiel on 7 December 1941, the day of infamy when the US entered the war after the attack on Pearl Harbor. This two week patrol ended when *U-86* entered Brest to join the 1st Flotilla. The crew were given practically no time to get used to their new surroundings; they celebrated Christmas ashore and just two days later were back at sea again, heading for the Canadian seaboard.

Success was not long in coming: the U-boat joined a wolf pack and in the early afternoon of 16 January the British 8,627 ton ship

USS *BOGUE*

USS *CARD*

Toorak was torpedoed while sailing with convoy ON52. The merchant ship did not sink, but nevertheless it was a good beginning. In the early hours of the morning, two days later, convoy SC63 was attacked by the pack which included Ali Cremer in *U-333*. The first ship, a Greek 4,271 ton steamer *Dimitrios G. Thormiotis*, fell victim to *U-86* when it was sunk by torpedo. The wireless operator on the steamer managed to transmit an 'attacked by U-boat' signal before his ship plunged to its fate. The distress signal was heard by the telegraphist on *U-86* and was also picked up by *U-552* which at the time was tracking another victim.

At the beginning of February *U-86* fired a three-torpedo salvo at a convoy at dawn, two detonations were heard after a ten minute wait but disappointingly for the crew they were end of range explosions. The U-boat set sail for its Brittany base and arrived back the day after St Valentine's day. The crew had earned their leave and after six weeks ashore were back at sea for a two month patrol off the American eastern seaboard which turned out to be most disappointing with no sinkings achieved. The fourth patrol, to the North Atlantic, was hardly much more successful. At dusk on 7 August a small American sailing vessel was sunk by the guns crew and *U-86* itself was slightly damaged by T-Tommy of 58 Squadron before arriving back at base on 18 September.

After six weeks ashore, *U-86*'s crew were again at sea on the last day of October; this time the patrol area was to the west of Gibraltar and off the Azores. No successes had been achieved by Christmas Eve when the U-boat rendezvoused with the Type XIV milch-cow *U-463* in mid-Atlantic. Besides the usual fuel replenishment the supply boat passed over a Metox GSR aerial. Later the use of this type of aerial was banned as the Allies were D/Fing their transmissions. In the short term the aerial did not assist *U-86* which returned on 7 January with no sinking to report.

The next patrol, which began on 24 February, covered the crucial convoy battles of March, but despite the huge German successes of the wolf packs *U-86* did not achieve any sinkings. On 11 March Kapitänleutnant Horst Dieterichs in *U-406* recorded hits on the 5,464 ton British steamer *Jamaica Producer* in convoy HX228. Kapitänleutnant Walter Schug also reported hits on the same ship by FAT's. When the steamer was brought into harbour the damage

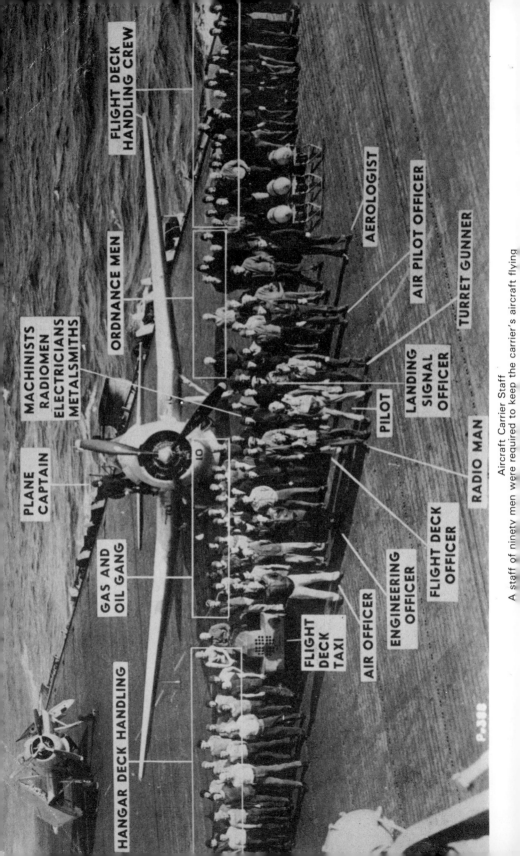

FLIGHT DECK HANDLING CREW

ORDNANCE MEN

MACHINISTS
RADIOMEN
ELECTRICIANS
METALSMITHS

PLANE CAPTAIN

GAS AND OIL GANG

HANGAR DECK HANDLING

AEROLOGIST

AIR PILOT OFFICER

TURRET GUNNER

LANDING SIGNAL OFFICER

PILOT

RADIO MAN

FLIGHT DECK OFFICER

ENGINEERING OFFICER

AIR OFFICER

FLIGHT DECK TAXI

Aircraft Carrier Staff

A staff of ninety men were required to keep the carrier's aircraft flying was reported as from 'internal explosions'.

The boat returned to Brest on 16 April and remained in port during the U-boat holocaust of May. In fact *U-86* did not commence its seventh patrol until 8 July when it carried out yet another unproductive two month patrol off the West African coast, returning on 11 September. The crew went home for what was to be their last leave.

For its eighth war patrol *U-86* was allocated a search area between Spain and the Azores. It was Thursday 11 November when Kapitänleutnant Walter Schug conned his U-boat out of Brest for the seventh time. The weather was rough and he had to be careful to avoid the violent seas off the towering headlands of the Point du Raz and Cap de la Chèvre. The U-boat successfully completed the passage through the Bay and on the 28th signalled to U-boat headquarters that it was in position 320 miles east-north-east of the Azores. The next day it was sunk by aircraft from *Bogue*.

The carrier had four aircraft in the air. Sharp-eyed pilot Lieutenant Bernard Volm sighted *U-86* fully surfaced and immediately had a sighting report sent off to *Bogue*. The other three aircraft were vectored to the scene and three others were launched. The experienced Lieutenant H. G. Bradshaw made the initial attack, closely followed by Volm and the two other Avengers. Two explosions were seen, but on the carrier it was not considered that the U-boat had been sunk.

However, nothing more was ever heard or seen of *U-86* and so the aircraft from *Bogue* have been credited with its sinking. The U-boat was just nine days short of two years' service at sea on eight active patrols.

Two weeks later, still on the same patrol, *Bogue* and her escorts landed a very big fish; *U-172* a Type IXC boat that had been responsible for the loss of 26 Allied ships.

The U-boat had been launched from the A. G. Weser yard at Bremen on 5 August 1941 and was commissioned by Karl Emmermann. The first war cruise was an eleven day shakedown one which took the boat to Lorient, 'the base of the aces' home of the 10th Flotilla on the River Scorfe.

The boat did not remain long in the French base, for eight days later its captain conned it through the narrows and into the Bay of Biscay, en route to the Caribbean. Once it arrived on station success came thick and fast for *U-172*. On the night of 27 May the first victim, torpedoed and gunned, was the British 8,940 ton motor tanker *Athel Knight*. Five nights later an American 5,447 ton steamer *Illinois* was torpedoed and sunk. Two nights later another American steamer, *Delfina*, of 3,480 tons was also torpedoed and sunk. Three nights later on 8 June a small American motor ship, *Sicilien*, was torpedoed. In the morning of 14 June another American steamer, the 8,289 ton *Lebore*, was torpedoed. The following evening a small Norwegian steamer, *Bennestvet*, was sunk. Three days later, in the early hours the guns' crew were given more practice and they sank the *Motorex*, a small American motor tanker. On the 23rd a small Colombian sailing ship was sunk. The last victim of the patrol was the 8,379 ton steamer *Santa Rita* which was sunk to the east of the West Indies on the afternoon of 9 July, but it took artillery fire as well as torpedoes to sink the American ship.

Commander Karl Emmermann had a mixed bag of successes to report when he arrived back at Lorient on 21 July after completing his Caribbean patrol: a total of nine ships sunk varying in size from the 35 ton sailing ship to a steamer of nearly 9,000 tons.

The crew only spent a month ashore before embarking on their third war patrol, and a long one it was to be. Setting out in mid-summer on 19 August they would not return until mid-winter, just after Christmas. This time the operational area was the Atlantic narrows. After a mid-ocean refuelling *U-172* arrived off Capetown and during the night of 7 October the 6,200 ton American steamer *Chickasaw City* was torpedoed and sunk. In the same area, just over four hours later and in daylight, the Panamanian ship *Firethorn* of 4,700 tons became the next victim. Amazingly on the very next morning, in the early hours a Greek steamer *Pantelis*, of just under 4,000 tons, was sunk nearby. In this same area, off South Africa, Karl Merten in *U-68* and Helmutt Witte in *U-159* were also registering successes. Off the Cape, at mid-morning on 10 October, *U-172* sank the troop carrier *Orcades*. The sinking of the 23,456 ton British liner was the highlight of Karl Emmermann's career. The loss of this fine ship and the 20,000 ton *Duchess of Atholl* by *U-178* a couple of hours earlier and the *Oronsay* the previous day was a

Grumman aircraft on deck

grievous blow to the British. Their only compensation was that there were comparatively few casualties. During the next couple of weeks *U-172* moved away from the coast westwards until on the last day of October the British motorship *Aldington Court* of just under 5,000 tons became the next victim when it was torpedoed in a night attack.

The U-boats operating in the Capetown-Durban area sank 24 ships totalling over 161,000 tons during the month. The Admiralty were compelled to reinforce the escorts in the area and sent out twenty ships, of which a dozen were trawlers from the Western Approaches.

In the dark evening of 2 November the unsuspecting British steamer *Llandilo* of nearly 5,000 tons was torpedoed and sunk west of the Cape, but it was three weeks before the next victim came into periscope view. By this time *U-172* was on its way home and had just crossed the Equator when the British 6,630 ton steamer *Benlomond* came into view in the early afternoon; it was torpedoed and sunk. The last victim of the patrol was caught in mid-ocean between South America and Africa on 28 November and in a dawn attack the guns' crew were given some practice after a torpedo had failed to sink the American steamer *Alaskan* of 5,364 tons.

The U-boat, now running short of fuel, was directed to a mid-Atlantic supply rendezvous. The crew could hardly believe their eyes; here in mid-Atlantic were seven U-boats and the milch-cow Type XIV supply boat. Among those present were Ernst Bauer with *U-126*, Albrecht Achilles with *U-161*, Ulrich Thilo with *U-174*, Helmut Witte with *U-159* and Ulrich Heyse with *U-128*. Witte and Emmermann were friends, having been together in the 1934 class, and they both visited Ulrich Heyse in *U-128*; he had graduated a year earlier.

Owing to stormy weather in the Bay of Biscay Karl Emmermann just failed to return in time for Christmas, arriving on 27 December. He and his crew were not called on again for another two months and lost no time in going ashore to make up for the five months they had spent at sea. During mid-January Allied bombers laid waste large parts of Lorient, with night raids, but *U-172* was safe in the bunkers, and many of the crew were on home leave in Germany.

The fourth war patrol commenced on 21 February and the crew were relieved to hear it was to be to the eastern seaboard of the

United States. In a dawn attack, in mid-Atlantic, on 4 March the British steamer *City of Pretoria* was sunk by *U-172* and later in the day, and in the same area, *U-515* sank another ship of a similar size, 8,000 tons. A night victim of *U-172* two days later was the 3,000 ton Norwegian motorship *Thorstrand*. March was the month that cost the Allies 108 ships with 627,000 lost tonnage. A week after its last attack *U-172* joined with a pack that attacked UGS6, a slow convoy from the United States to Gibraltar. In a night attack Emmermann sank *Keystone* and three days later, the 16th, in an evening attack *U-172* fired a four-torpedo spread which resulted in the sinking of *Benjamin Harrison*. Both victims had been American steamers of 5,500 and 7,000 tons respectively. Freiherr Walter von Steinaecker in *U-524* was another to record a success against the convoy. Nearly a fortnight later *U-172*, with *U-167* and *U-159*, fell upon convoy RS3 from Gibraltar to Sierra Leone and sank *Silverbeach*, a British 5,000 tonner, just after midnight on 29 November. It was time to return to base.

The U-boat spent six weeks in Lorient before commencing its fifth war cruise, the last with Karl Emmermann in command. On 29 May he conned *U-172* out of the river Scorfe into the Bay of Biscay for a new patrol area, off the South American coast. South of the Equator, midway across the South Atlantic, between South America and Africa, the British 4,748 ton British steamer *Vernon City* was sunk in a dawn attack on 28 June. The next day a message was sent to *U-172* and *U-185* to proceed to a position off Pernambuco to rescue the crew of *U-604*. The Type VIIC boat on its sixth war patrol had been depth-charged by US aircraft and the destroyer *Moffet*. Although badly damaged, *U-604* attempted to return to base. When this was found to be impossible the boat was scuttled and the crew rescued by *U-172* and *U-185*. The now overcrowded U-boat continued with its patrol and on another dawn attack off the Brazilian coast on 12 July torpedoed and sank the American steamer *African Star* of 6,500 tons. Three days later and further out to sea Emmermann sank the British 4,000 ton ship *Harmonic* at dusk. Nine days later, on 24 July, in another dusk attack *U-172* sank its last victim, a 7,000 ton British steamer *Fort Chilcotin*.

Now *U-172* was on its way back to Lorient, there is no doubt that the crew were anxious to shake off their sea-legs after spending all the summer at sea, and so on 7 September Karl Emmermann took his boat into Lorient for the last time. In a space of fourteen months he had sent 26 Allied ships to the bottom and earned himself the Knight's Cross with Oak Leaves. After having been a Lorient boat for all its previous commissions *U-172* now moved to St Nazaire - not only was there a new base, but there was a new commander, Oberleutnant Hermann Hoffmann. Also, when the boat set off on Monday 22 November for its sifth war patrol, there was a new operational area, the Indian Ocean. The boat was one of the three of the larger ones sent to the distant operational area. The instructions were to remain unseen and not to attack targets until the patrol area was reached. On 30 November *U-172* signalled in, confirming its safe passage through the Bay of Biscay and into the Atlantic. It was the last message received by U-boat headquarters. Almost a fortnight later, when 180 miles south-west of the Canary Islands and 600 miles north-north-west of Cape Verde, *U-172* inadvertently came too close to convoy GUS23 crossing from Casablanca back to the United States. Worse still the carrier *Bogue* was in the vicinity of the convoy with, in turn, its escort of USS *George E Badger*, *Dupont*, *Clemson* and *George W. Ingram*.

On 11 December *U-219* had already replenished three boats but the lines were still attached to *U-172* when aircraft from *Bogue* were sighted. The auxiliary tanker quickly submerged but *U-172* was still on the surface and the hunt was on. The U-boat submerged immediately and *Clemson* was ordered to the spot. On arrival asdic contact was established and a depth pattern dropped. While this was being done a carrier borne aircraft patrol overhead looked for telltale signs of destruction.

The other escorts steamed to join *Clemson* hunting *U-172*. Down below the U-boat crew were observing silent routine; the motors were cut, the crew lay down wherever there was a space. It was a cat and mouse game with the hunters knowing that their quarry would have to surface eventually for air and to charge the batteries. The escorts waited throughout the day and into the night. How long could the U-boat remain submerged. Although lying deep the U-boat was located time and again by the destroyers and each time another pattern of depth charges were dropped. The U-boat was unable to escape the unwelcome attention of its attackers and sheer desperation caused its new commander to surface in the early hours of 12 December. The crew needed air and the batteries needed charging. As soon as the U-boat's silhouette was seen all hell was let loose; the destroyers opened fire with their guns and as *U-172* scrambled below, depth charges were released. It was the beginning of the end. The U-boat's pressure hull was damaged and *U-172* was fatally leaking oil.

As dawn broke the Wildcats from *Bogue* were back again. Just after 0800 Lieutenant H. G. Bradshaw spotted the telltale oil slick and radioed the information to the ships below. It was now nearly all over. The asdic was superfluous; the oil leaking to the surface gave away *U-172*'s position. The depth charges rained down from *Clemson* and *Ingram* but still the U-boat couldn't or wouldn't surface. The depth charges were running short and by mid-morning there was no sign of the Germans giving up the struggle.

Then it happened, a quick rise to the surface and a run for it. It was really no contest. As soon as *U-172* broke through, it was seen by an excited pilot who communicated his delight in clear.

Two more flights were scrambled from the flight deck of the carrier and together the three aircraft strafed the U-boat, machine-gunning the conning tower. Some of the submariners were knocked, or jumped, into the sea. The aircraft veered off, thinking the crew were abandoning *U-172*, but it was not so.

Other crewmen manned the guns and the U-boat opened fire. One shell struck *Ingram*'s quarterdeck, killing one and injuring eight members of the crew. The one sided fight could have only one end, but the crew of *U-172* kept firing. The gunnery from the American destroyers was soon on target and *U-172* was drifting helplessly round in circles. In six minutes its deck was awash and the crew poured out of the conning tower as it plunged for the last time.

Oberleutnant Hermann Hoffmann, his 1WO and 33 of the crew were rescued. *Bogue* and her escorts had scored another victory.

Klaus Ewert was a veteran U-boat commander, from the class of 1925. At the commencement of the war he was commander of *U-26* and within three months sank a Belgian, Dutch and Greek ship off the British coast. By the end of 1942 the Kapitänleutnant that was had been promoted to Fregattenkapitän; this was a high rank for a

U-boat commander but commanders going East sometimes also needed diplomatic skills when visiting Japanese bases. Boats going East could no longer refuel en route as all the supply ships had been sunk and in consequence they had to make the Japanese-held Penang.

The new boat Laus Ewert took over was the Type IXD₂ *U-850*, launched from the slip of A. G. Weser at Bremen.

It was almost a year after launching before *U-850* set out from Kiel, on 18 November. By 29 December, on its way to the Indian Ocean it had reached a position west of Madeira and nearly six hundred miles south of the Azores. Early on that Monday afternoon as the surfaced U-boat made its way, at 15 knots, through the South Atlantic under the hot sun and cloudless blue sky, the lookouts were less than vigilant and this lack of concentration was to cost them and the crew their lives.

Lieutnant W. A. LaFleur, flying an Avenger from *Bogue*, sighted *U-850* from six miles. He immediately commenced a depth charge run and at the same time had a signal transmitted giving a contact report to the carrier that was less than seventy miles away. The first run caught *U-850* by surprise; no shots were fired as the attack commenced but the depth charges would not release. The pilot turned and made a second run on the now fully alerted U-boat. The guns were manned and a short 'am being attacked by aircraft' report was sent to U-boat headquarters as the Avenger came in at 300 feet on its second run. This time the depth charges released but fell short. The pilot still had a Mark 24 mine aboard, but as this homing torpedo could only be dropped once the U-boat had submerged, he decided to remain within range in order to be in a position to employ his weapon if the opportunity arose.

Meanwhile there was a flurry of activity aboard *Bogue*. Immediately on receipt of the contact report two more Avengers and two Wildcats were catapulted off to the scene. One Avenger was loaded with four depth charges and the other, flown by Lieutenant Bradshaw who had attacked *U-172*, was equipped with two depth charges and a homing torpedo. When the quartet arrived *U-850* was too preoccupied firing at its original attacker to notice them; once again the lookouts were failing in their duty. Unobserved, the Wildcats screamed into the attack and began pumping bullets into the U-boat's deck. Only then did *U-850* commence firing at its new attackers. The fighters strafed the decks, stopping firing from all but two guns. The Avenger then planted its depth charges accurately from 150 feet. The first landed ten feet off the starboard bow, the second hit the U-boat near the conning tower, the third exploded fifteen feet off the port beam and the last exploded forty feet off the port quarter.

The U-boat was completely enveloped in spray, and upon its subsidence, *U-850* was observed moving on course but trailing a large amount of oil. Lieutenant Bradshaw now came in at 75 feet and releases his two depth charges, which landed 200 feet off the U-boat's port bow. While his Avenger was making its run, the two Wildcats wheeled and commenced a second strafing run on the starboard quarter. One pilot saw his tracers strike the base of the conning tower aft and observed a bright flash of flame shoot from the area, leading him to believe that he had hit the ready use ammunition locker.

As the fighters were making this strafing attack *U-850* started a crash dive. The fighters turned and made a third strafing run on the stern about thirty seconds later. As the U-boat was observed starting its dive the two Avengers carrying homing torpedoes commenced their runs. Lieutenant Bradshaw made a direct up-track approach and his mine struck about 200 feet ahead of the swirl and 100 feet to the right of the track. Lieutenant LaFleur dropped his mine 250 feet ahead of the swirl and 125 feet to the right of the track from 150 feet.

The U-boat started to re-surface, its bow breaking the surface at a sharp angle, just as the second mine hit the water. Then the first mine struck the U-boat's stern on the starboard side and a split second later the other one hit the starboard side midway between the conning tower and the stern. The two explosions merged into one very heavy blast, which threw the stern high in the air, scattering debris in all directions. The stern disintegrated under the blast and the U-boat immediately sank bow up at a vertical angle. The fighters made a fourth strafing run during and immediately after the explosion. Less than half-an-hour had elapsed from the first sighting to the destruction of *U-850*.

Escort destroyers USS *Badger* and *Dupont* arrived at the scene three-and-a-half hours later. They reported picking up pieces of wood, life jackets, pieces of clothing and dismembered bodies.

This was the third sinking of the cruise from *Bogue*'s task group which ended in America on New Year's Eve. The U-boat was the third of the boats sent to reinforce the strength in the Indian Ocean to be sunk in a month.

Four days after *Bogue*'s hunter-killers' success another anti-U-boat task force, built around the carrier *Card*, was searching for marauding Atlantic U-boats. The U-boat to fall to them was *U-645*, a Hamburg-built Type VIIC boat launched from the Blohm and Voss yard at the beginning of September 1942. Reserve officer Oberleutnant Otto Ferro was given command of the boat.

The morale of the U-boatmen was high by the time *U-645* was due to leave Kiel for its first war patrol on 24 April. The Atlantic U-boats had achieved major successes on the convoy routes the previous month. The patrol, which ended at Brest on 22 June, was notable only for the fact that *U-645* had survived the slaughter of Atlantic U-boats in May and was one of the few not to be recalled by Admiral Dönitz at the end of the month.

The second patrol, again to the North Atlantic, commenced from the Brittany port on 23 August. A month later, on 20 September, *U-645* gave the *coup de grâce* to a 7,000 ton American steamer *Frederick Douglass* which had been torpedoed by *U-238* earlier in the day. Three days later *U-645* was one of a nineteen-strong U-boat pack in a patrol line waiting to attack convoy ONS19. The Allies, who were reading U-boat control signals at the time, successfully diverted the convoy round the waiting U-boats.

On 7 October *U-645* was included in a signal addressed to sixteen U-boats to intercept the heavily escorted eastbound convoy SC143. Only one ship in the convoy was sunk and this by *U-645* on 9th when the American 5,612 ton steamer *Yorkmar* was torpedoed in a dawn attack. Five U-boats had been lost for this sinking and that of a destroyer, and immediately after the success by *U-645* the pack was ordered to break off the attack and move westwards as the convoy was within range of UK-based aircraft.

At the end of the patrol *U-645* again returned to Brest but before commencing its next patrol, on 2 December, it moved down to La

Pallice. The designated patrol area was between Spain and the Azores. The U-boat radioed in its position on 12 December and by Christmas Eve it was in a position 460 miles north-east of the Azores when it was intercepted.

The American task force, led by Captain 'Buster' Isbell in *Card*, was being tossed about in the 'foam blown grey North Atlantic waves' when suddenly in the dreaded first watch the asdic operator in the destroyer *Schenck* picked up a radar contact.

The seas were wind-whipped and icy but at 0216, with the range at just over 10,000 yards, the operator was convinced that the 'pip' was that of a U-boat contact. Lieutenant-Commander Logsdon rushed for the spot and ordered a sighting report to be transmitted. The contact faded on the screen as the bow of the destroyer cut through the icy sea. The depth charge party were at the ready on the stern as were the rest of the crew, many of them aroused from their slumber by the sounds of the Action Station alarm, and many of them were going into battle for the first time. The ship's engineers were coaxing all they could from their Thornycroft boilers and were rewarded when, at 2,500 yards, the U-boat was sighted in the act of submerging, its stern towards the destroyer.

This was a dangerous moment for a pursuer; it was the time the U-boat would order a homing torpedo to be fired. The destroyer captain shifted his rudder after swinging fifty degrees and slowed down to fifteen knots.

The asdic was switched on and contact made at 240 feet. Less than 35 minutes after Action Stations had sounded the first charges of a pattern were being dropped. *Schenck* rolled and veered as fountains of water cascaded in her wake.

After half-an-hour of depth-charging the radar operator picked up a contact at 4,000 yards, *U-645* was making a run on the surface. The destroyer turned on to the bearing and the pursuit was on. When the range had closed to 2,500 yards radar contact was lost, *U-645* had submerged again. It was a mistake, the last Otto Ferro was to make. There was no chance of the crew being saved from below.

Asdic contact was established and at 0327 *Schenck* despatched another depth-charge pattern. Two minutes after the charges were fired a rumbling blast welled up from the deep with a detonation that shook the destroyer, nearly deafening the asdic operator. Those up top saw a great billow of oil spurt up. The oil covered the sea and there was the unmistakable smell of diesel. Although the captain was certain of his kill he had just given an order for a bucket to be trailed over the side to secure a sample when an urgent message was received. The destroyer *Leary* had been torpedoed. Confirmation of the sinking of *U-645* was forgotten as *Schenck* put on full speed and rushed back to protect *Card*.

While *Schenck* had been away a pack had located the task force. At 0143 Kurt Neide in *U-415* fired one three-torpedo FAT spread, but missed its intended target, *Card*, and also the accompanying destroyer *Decatur*. Just after 0500 Helmut Bork in *U-275* fired a gnat which hit *Leary*. Rudolf Zorn, in *U-382*, also fired a gnat at the destroyer but this did not hit, probably because its propellers were not making enough noise to attract the torpedo. However, the first hit was enought to sink the destroyer.

The result of the task force versus the wolf pack could probably be considered as a draw. The sinking of *U-645* proved to be the last of 1943 and in fact started a lull of over a fortnight, as if a truce had been declared over the festive season.

Continuing with American auxiliary carriers, but jumping ahead to January 1944, we come to USS *Guadalcanal*, of 7,800 tons, which was built on the hull of a merchant ship by the Henry Kaiser shipbuilding company of Vancouver, Washington State. The escort carrier was commissioned at the US naval base at Astoria, Oregon on 25 September 1943 and was the first Kaiser-built carrier to appear in the Atlantic.

Captain Daniel V. Gallery commissioned the ship which had a crew with an average age of 21, of which only one-fifth had ever previously been to sea. As every crew member joined the new carrier he was handed a memorandum, signed by the captain, which read:

1.   The motto of the *Guadalcanal* will be 'Can Do', meaning that we will take any tough job that is handed to us and run away with it. The tougher the job the better we'll like it.

2.   Before a carrier can do its big job of sinking enemy ships

USS *Guadalcanal* . . .
. . . and certificate that holder served aboard the carrier

several hundred small unspectacular jobs have got to be done, and done well. One man falling down on a small job can 'bitch the works' for the whole ship. So learn everything you can about your job during this pre-commissioning period. Pretty soon we will be out where it rains bombs, and it will be too late to learn then. *Note.* This ship will be employed on dangerous duty. We will either sink the enemy or get sunk ourselves, depending on how well we learn our jobs now and do our jobs later. Anyone who prefers safer duty see me, and I will arrange to have him transferred.

Following the shakedown cruise and training exercises off the west coast, *Guadalcanal*, in company with the escort carrier *Mission Bay* and the destroyer *Welles*, steamed out of San Diego harbour on 15 November bound for Norfolk, Virginia, via the Panama Canal, arriving on 3 December. Last minute repairs and calibrations were made, ammunition loaded and composite squadron 13 came onboard.

When the air group joined the carrier they were made to feel welcome as part of the ship's crew. This had not always been so and the captain, as an ex-naval pilot, made it his duty to see the aviators were integrated.

While in Norfolk Dan Gallery took the opportunity of talking with Captain A. J. Isbell, captain of *Card*, a former classmate. *Card* had served in the Atlantic for many months sinking U-boats, and the captain of the new carrier was able to benefit from the knowledge gained by the experienced *Card* captain.

On 5 January the task force, consisting of *Guadalcanal* and her escorts, left for Norfolk and got underway for the first co-ordinated anti-U-boat patrol along the US/Gibraltar convoy route, with just an overnight stop in Bermuda to refuel. The first war cruise got off to a bad start when one of the most experienced pilots was killed, crashing while landing on the carrier.

Better news was to follow for the Americans, on the evening of 16 January, when *U-544* was caught on the surface. The U-boat was a large new one, a Type IXC$_{40}$ built at the Deutsche Werft in Hamburg and launched on 17 February 1943 under the command of the high-ranking Korvettenkapitän Willy Mattke.

After Baltic trials and exercises *U-544* left Kiel on 9 November for its first and only patrol. The U-boat was sent to the North Atlantic to report twice daily on the weather conditions. The boat was also used as an auxiliary refueller and before returning to base was ordered to replenish *U-516* and *U-129*. The homeward-bound U-boat met the other boats about 360 miles west-north-west of the Azores on 16 January, four days after it had transmitted its last message to U-boat Control.

For one of the U-boats, *U-129* a Type IXC boat, this was the second consecutive occasion that it had to refuel in mid-ocean from an auxiliary boat. On its eighth war cruise out of Lorient to the West Indies area in the summer it had to abandon its task due to the loss of its refueller and take on fuel from another U-boat before it was able to return to base. Now, on its ninth patrol, which had started from St Nazaire on 12 October to the coast of Florida, the same thing had happened and it was routed to meet *U-544*.

The other boat, *U-516*, also a Type IXC, had left Brest on 4 October and had sunk six ships on this, its fourth, patrol. On a previous operation in the summer it had been used as an auxiliary refueller itself, replenishing other boats in mid-Atlantic.

Unfortunately for the Germans, the position they chose for their rendezvous was only twenty miles from the task force. At 1845, on 16 January, just before sunset, eight aircraft returning from patrol were scheduled to land on *Guadalcanal*. Just twenty minutes to touchdown, two aircraft on their return leg to the carrier could hardly believe their luck when three surfaced U-boats were seen below. They quickly concluded that there was a refuelling operation in progress and acted accordingly. Solid overcast made it easy for them to approach unseen. Rockets and depth charges plastered the U-boats, encumbered as they were with tow-lines and fuel hoses. One, *U-516*, managed to disentangle itself and submerged. The other, *U-129*, hard alongside, was not so fortunate and was badly damaged. Poor *U-544* had no chance and it quickly sank. The other aircraft couldn't resist the opportunity and instead of landing flew over to the scene of the action, a decision which was to cost them dearly. The carrier had just swung into the wind to land the aircraft on, when the U-boats were spotted. By the time they returned it was getting dark. The first four landed on successfully but the fifth landed too far to the right and blocked the landing area and fouled the arrester gear. The deck crew were unable to move the crashed aircraft and the sixth aircraft was ordered to land on the other side of the carrier's deck. The result was predictable. After a dozen 'wave offs' it came in much too fast, hit the deck, skidded, bounced and rolled over into the sea. The captain then ordered the remaining two aircraft to land on the sea. The rescue of the airmen was extremely dangerous, as most of the ships did not want to stop with U-boats known to be in the area.

In the meantime a destroyer had been detached to search for the thirty survivors seen in the water in a pool of *U-544*'s oil and wreckage. It was a very black and windy night and no sign of the attack was found when the destroyers reached the approximate area. Once again, because of the prospect of U-boat attacks, the would-be rescuers were unable to use any lights for fear of giving away their positions, so the captain and his crew all perished.

Next day back aboard *Guadalcanal* when all reports had been analysed two U-boats were claimed destroyed and two German flags were painted on the side of the carrier's bridge to signify the sinkings. The Americans were over-optimistic as *U-129* limped into Lorient on 31 January and the severely damaged *U-516* reached the same base on 26 February.

USS *Guadalcanal* had sunk *U-544* but had lost four aircraft. Following the attack, on its next patrol in the Atlantic, the carrier redressed the balance by sinking the very experienced *U-515* and *U-68* on successive days in April, rescuing Kapitänleutnant Werner Henke and 43 of his crew and one from *U-68*. The event for which Dan Gallery is best known was the capture, in June, of *U-505* which is now on display in Chicago.

The US 'Woolworth' carriers certainly played their part in the defeat of the wolf packs.

CHAPTER SIX

Full Circle

When the Germans occupied the French Atlantic coast they took over the ports of Brest, Lorient, St Nazaire, La Pallice and Bordeaux as U-boat bases. Admiral Dönitz, then the U-boat commander, conducted a personal survey of the five ports before selecting Lorient for his headquarters. On the north bank of the River Blauet he converted a château at Kerneval into a command post. The château was next to an eighteenth-century stone fort that guarded the entrance to the river and afforded a clear view past Port Louis, over the harbour and the U-boat quays. When the Admiral moved from Paris to his new headquarters in September 1940 work had already begun on the foundations of the massive shelters that were being built by construction workers of the Todt Organization to protect the U-boats from air raid attacks. At the same time a command bunker was being built in the garden of the château so that the headquarters staff could retire there to escape Allied air attacks, as Kerneval was within easy reach of English airfields.

While all this construction work was continuing apace, Gerd Kelbling, who had joined the Kriegsmarine as an eighteen-year-old, was serving in a minesweeping flotilla. Born in Salzbrunn Schlesien, on 12 June 1915 he was in the officers' class of 1934. After general service he was serving in a river auxiliary minesweeper when war was declared. He joined the minesweeping flotilla in November 1939 and remained with it for fourteen months before commencing a five month U-boat training course in January 1941. He then spent two months' consolidation with the 24th U-boat Flotilla at Danzig before getting the chance to go to sea aboard *U-557*, which was under the command of his classmate Ottokar Paulshen, who had already distinguished himself by sinking the 7,290 ton British steamer *Empire Storm* on 29 May, while in a convoy.

Kapitänleutnant Gerd Kelbling joined *U-557* early one August afternoon with what was almost a pier-head jump; he boarded the Type VIIC boat just half-an-hour before it left Lorient on its second war patrol. The commander was pleased to have him aboard as he was a supernumerary, sailing as a prospective commanding officer; what valuable experience it was to prove.

Almost as soon as Gerd Kelbling was aboard the ropes were cast off from their bollards and *U-557* was moving. This was at the time when bands played at the departure, the command staff assembled to see each boat off and when new girlfriends waited at the end of the quay to see off their sailormen.

The majority of the crew were on deck to return the waves and enjoy their last view of the sky for a few days. The sun was high in the sky as the electric motors drove the U-boat into the river just after 1400. The diesels spluttered into life as *U-557* came into view of those looking out from the command château at Kerneval. Out past Port Louis on the far bank, through the buoyed approaches, into the grey waves of the Bay of Biscay, with just the escort vessel for company. As the port and the Brittany coastline disappeared from view, the escort boat's captain wished his opposite number good luck and departed. The ratings went below, leaving just Paulshen and Kelbling on deck. The U-boat was conned through a fleet of multi-coloured French fishing trawlers. Once through the boats the commander ordered, 'Both full ahead' and together with Kelbling he went below. The obligatory trim dive was then carried out. Gerd Kelbling was at sea on his first war patrol and *U-557* on its second. This time its initial patrol area was to the south-west of Ireland. The crew were called to Action Stations several times during the patrol and from wireless intercepts it was obvious that other U-boats were registering successes; *U-557*, not too far from the scene of action was picked up and received a pattern of depth charges.

It was not until the early hours of 27 August, when west of central Ireland, that the first victims of the patrol were sunk. A convoy bound for the United Kingdom from Freetown was intercepted and in a space of nine minutes the Norwegian motorship *Segundo* of 4,414 tons was torpedoed and sunk; the British steamer *Saugor* of 6,303 tons was to follow shortly. The tubes were quickly reloaded and forty minutes after the first salvo the 4,736 ton British steamer *Tremoda* followed the earlier victims to the bottom of the sea. The tubes were again reloaded and some two hours later the British ship *Embassage* of just under five thousand tons passed the cross wires of the periscope. The torpedoes were fired and the steamer became the fourth victim of the night and the patrol, for the last two torpedoes fired at the convoy were failures. U-boat headquarters was notified of the night's successes and *U-557* kept with the convoy for three hours while other U-boats homed. Among these boats was *U-558*, the next off the production line, launched from the Blohm and Voss slip at Hamburg just one day after *U-557*; later in the day this boat was to sink a British motorship of over ten thousand tons. Once the pack had joined, the patrol of *U-557* was at an end. Course was shaped for the Bay of Biscay and Lorient.

The prospective commanding officer had learned much, to recognise and navigate through a fishing fleet, how to carry out a trim dive, experienced depth-charging, assisted four sinkings and witnessed the homing procedure and the releasing of beacons to call other U-boats. Gerd Kelbling was now ready to take over his own boat. He left *U-557* none too soon, for it was sunk within three months.

The U-boat Gerd Kelbling was to command, *U-593*, a Type VIIC, was launched on 3 September 1941; also from the Blohm and Voss yard at Hamburg; it was the second anniversary of the outbreak of war.

After the watch officers had been selected and the ratings drafted, Gerd Kelbling knocked them into shape in the Baltic training area and they were released as an active service boat, ready for their first war cruise at the beginning of March 1942.

The laborious task of loading torpedoes, ammunition and fuel completed, *U-593* proceeded from Kiel-Wik on its first war patrol on 2 March 1942.

The U-boat was ordered to patrol off the Irish coast before proceeding to join the 7th Flotilla at St Nazaire at the end of the month.

Unknown to Gerd Kelbling, or indeed anybody in Germany, the Royal Navy also intended to be at St Nazaire at the end of March.

In Britain the Admiralty, concerned that *Tirpitz* was now operational, planned to make sure that neither this nor any other capital ship could dock at a French base after any Atlantic foray. The only dry-dock available and large enough to accommodate such a ship was at St Nazaire where it had been constructed to hold the French trans-Atlantic liner *Normandie*.

A plan, approved by the Chiefs of Staff, was for a combined operations attack on the outer cassion of the dock and commando raids on other installations.

The code name for the raid was Operation Chariot and at the time the bold plan was known as 'The greatest raid of all'. Simply the plan was for a ship, packed with explosives in its bows and having a delayed time setting, to ram the lock gates thereby rendering the dry dock useless.

Commander R. E. D. Ryder was in charge of the naval operation and had at his disposal the ex-American destroyer *Campbeltown*, which had her funnels cut down to resemble a German torpedo boat of the Möwe class. *Campbeltown* was to be expended as the ramming ship. The Hunt class destroyers *Atherstone* and *Tynedale*, with one MGB, sixteen MLs and one MTB, made up the attacking force. The light forces and *Campbeltown* carried the officers and men, demolition experts, and a covering force.

The timing of raid was so planned that *Campbeltown* could ride over the sandbanks of the River Loire on a spring tide. The striking force set sail from Falmouth on mid-afternoon of 26 March in order to reach its destination in the early hours of the 28th. *Atherstone* towed the MGB, which was being used as the headquarters ship, and *Campbeltown* towed the MTB. The first part of the 400 mile open-sea passage was successfully completed when the west Channel crossing was completed at 0100. Two French fishing trawlers were boarded and sunk as it was feared that they might notify the shore authorities of the presence of the force, but when the crews had been spoken to this was seen to be a false assumption and the remainder of the fleet were left to continue with their task.

Not far away *U-593* was nearing the end of its first operational war patrol, off Ireland. It had left Kiel 25 days earlier and its crew were looking forward to the delights offered at its new base of St Nazaire. Commander Gerd Kelbling looked at the plan of the harbour and saw that he would have to enter the harbour through the Avant Port, negotiate the south lock, before entering the Bassin du St Nazaire prior to securing alongside the wall near to where the U-boat pens were under construction. The Normandie dock was to the south of the basin.

At about 0700, in a position 110 miles south by west of the island of Ushant the British force reduced speed to eight knots and almost immediately *Tynedale* reported a suspicious object on the horizon to the north. Action stations were sounded and as the topmen reached their positions a U-boat, *U-593*, was seen surfacing. It had not been detected earlier because the asdic in *Tynedale* was defective.

Obviously *U-593*'s commander had scoured the horizon before surfacing, but he had little expected hostile ships to be so close to German-occupied territory and therefore there was no danger in surfacing two-and-a-half miles from the oncoming ship. The captain of *Tynedale* had quickly recognised the unsuspecting U-boat bow on; *U-593* fired a recognition signal of five white stars, and the reply from *Tynedale* was a depth charge pattern set to shallow. The U-boat quickly submerged but the depth charges caused it to break surface astern and as it did so it was shot up at close range and hit with pom-pom and machine-gun fire. The U-boat was then lost. *Atherstone* slipped its MGB and joined in the hunt.

For Commander Ryder the incident was potentially serious. The U-boat had obviously seen a destroyer, knew it was an enemy and once it had been reported might well bring out the five torpedo boats known to be based in St Nazaire; if this had happened it would have put paid to the raid.

While the destroyers hunted *U-593* Commander Ryder turned his force temporarily to the south-west, hoping that the Germans would think it was Mediterranean-bound.

After hunting unsuccessfully for two hours the destroyers were ordered to return to the main force and at 0939 the commander signalled to *Tynedale*:

> In one hour's time consider that a sighting report may have been made. Unless this is followed up by reconnaissance aircraft and further sighting, intend to continue with operation.

Tynedale replied:

Consider it unlikely that U-boat sighted MLs, possible enemy appreciation will be that we are two destroyers on passage to Gibraltar.

At 1400 *U-593* surfaced and reported the destroyers, but not the MLs. The German Naval Staff concluded that the destroyers were minelaying and, as a great bonus for the British, the five feared torpedo-boats were sent to sea at nightfall for a coastal patrol to seek them out.

It is now history that the naval part of the raid on the lock gates was carried out successfully but with many losses on both sides. The Germans were completely foxed as they did not conceive it credible that a British force could suddenly appear under their noses with such effrontery so far from home.

There was now nowhere in France that *Tirpitz* could dock. The object of the exercise had been successfully achieved. On the same day *U-593* arrived safely but the two protagonists were to meet again in twenty-one months' time, in a different theatre of operations. There were to be dire consequences for one of them as will be revealed shortly.

A strange side-effect to the British raid was that it precipitated the move of Admiral Dönitz's headquarters at Kerneval back to Paris. It was thought that a similar raid, on Lorient, could wipe out the U-boat command staff, whereas this was unlikely in the French capital. Karl Dönitz recorded in his war diary that this was a regrettable step since the direct contact with the front boats and their crews would not be possible to nearly the same extent. The move to Avenue Maréchal Maunoury in Paris took place on 29 March.

Once *U-593* had docked the German submariners quickly took the opportunity to explore their new surroundings while their commander reported to the 7th Flotilla headquarters. While there Gerd Kelbling was asked if he would like to inspect *Campbeltown*, which at that time was wedged tight into the lock gates. Fortunately for the U-boat commander he declined the invitation and at the same time probably saved his life, for when the delayed action fuse in the destroyer detonated – the explosion came some time after 1000 – the lock gates were demolished and many German officers who were looking over the former American ship were killed.

Things soon quietened down in St Nazaire as the last remnants of the attacking force were taken prisoner. The U-boat was taken in hand by the dockyard authorities to fix minor defects that had appeared on the first patrol and to check for damage following the depth charge attack by *Tynedale*. While this was going on the crew were accommodated in comfortable quarters in La Baule, a pleasant seaside resort, half-an-hour's drive from the port.

It was just over three weeks later that the good life ashore was cut short for the U-boat's crew. They put to sea on the Führer's 53rd birthday, 20 April, for their second patrol, to the happy hunting grounds off the American eastern seaboard.

At this time the first milch-cow, Type XIV *U-459*, refuelled fourteen U-boats north-east of Bermuda. The first two torpedoes aimed at an enemy leapt from their tubes in the early afternoon of 14 May when the Greek steamer *Stavros*, under charter, was hit in an area to the east of the coast of New Jersey. The torpedoes were seen to hit and *U-593* cleared the area. The 4,853 ton ship did not sink and was later salvaged. Another steamer was attacked in the early hours of 19th; two torpedoes were fired, but no hits resulted. A week later, in a dusk attack on the 25th, another ship was torpedoed in much the same area as the first attack. This attack was successful and the 8,426 ton Panamanian motor tanker *Persephone* went to the bottom of the ocean. So ended the second war patrol. It had lasted two months and *U-593* returned to St Nazaire on 18 June. The crew took local or home leave in two watches.

While *U-593* had been patrolling off the American coast, other U-boats in the area were engaged in different activities. Mines were laid off Boston, Delaware and Chesapeake Bay and two U-boats each landed four-man teams of saboteurs at Long Island and Florida.

The third patrol of *U-593* commenced on 22 July and the boat was still in the Bay of Biscay when Admiral Dönitz in a broadcast from Berlin described the ever increasing threat to U-boat operations from British and American sea and air forces, saying they were 'Always on the heels of our U-boats'.

After crossing the Atlantic *U-593* intercepted convoy SC94 and acted as watch-keeper until other boats homed in. In the early evening of 5 August *U-593* attacked and was the first U-boat to register a success. The weakly escorted convoy of 33 ships had left Canadian ports at the end of July and its movements had been picked by U-boat headquarters who had eighteen U-boats in the area waiting to attack; all but one of them were to have their chance.

The convoy had progressed to a position 450 miles south of Cape Farewell when *U-593* struck. Two ships were attacked and the Dutch ship *Spar*, of 3,616 tons, was seen to sink. A further hit was heard but no result was known. Fog at the land bases deprived the convoy of the air cover that Admiral Dönitz had complained about. In the course of the next few days *U-704*, *U-660*, *U-176*, *U-379*, *U-591*, *U-597* and *U-438* had all claimed successes but *U-379* itself was rammed and sunk, as was *U-210*. Eleven ships of the convoy, totalling 53,000 tons were sunk, two U-boats were lost and four others damaged. The 7th Flotilla boat suffered a defect and had to return to base, which was achieved without further difficulty on 19 August when Gerd Kelbling conned *U-593* into St Nazaire for the last time.

Six weeks later, with *U-593* repaired, the crew wished *auf Wiedersehen* to their comrades at the French base. Their boat was to join the 29th Flotilla in the Mediterranean. The U-boat left St Nazaire on 3 October and during the night of the 11/12th passed through the Straits of Gibraltar. This narrow configuration of water was cleared at 0425 after some very anxious moments of near detection, but *U-593* hid between Spanish fishing vessels, thus evading the RN patrols.

The U-boat had entered the Mediterranean none too soon, for on 8 November the Allies invaded North Africa and there were to be plenty of targets for the U-boats. In mid-afternoon of 12 November *U-593* fired two torpedo spreads north of Oran and heard detonations, but the Allies lost nothing. Soon after daybreak the next day *U-593* attacked an aircraft carrier and heard a detonation. Although it cannot be positively verified the carrier was probably HMS *Avenger* which was sunk by *U-155* during the night of the 14/15th not too far from the position where *U-593* had attacked.

The crew of *U-593* soon settled into their new surroundings, the only disappointment being a lack of targets at the beginning of 1943. On 3 March, just before midnight, not far off the coast of Libya,

U-593 fired at a small steamer and claimed a hit, though this could not be confirmed. On the morning of 18 March *U-593* sank two small British steamers off the Cyrenaican coast. Two more ships were attacked in exactly the same position in mid-afternoon of the 27th – a four torpedo spread was fired and three detonations were heard. The 5,157 ton British steamer *City of Guildford* was sunk and possibly another ship was hit. Returning to this happy hunting ground on 11 April Gerd Kelbling sank another small British steamer *Runo* just after midnight.

On 12 May all organised resistance in North Africa ended. Towards the end of June and at the beginning of July *U-593* sank *LSTs 333* and *387* and the British motorship *Devis*, of 6,000 tons, off Algiers. On 10 July the Allies invaded Sicily; at this time there were only eighteen German U-boats in the Mediterranean. The commander of one of these, Gerd Kelbling of *U-593* was awarded the Knight's Cross and the announcement was promulgated on 9 August. The commander was on leave at Lübeck at the time and he received a telegram ordering him to report to Kiel for the presentation to be made on 19 August. The award was for the achievements of himself, his crew and his boat so he requested the ceremony should take place at Toulon where his boat and his men were, however the prestigious presentation was made in Kiel.

By the time the Allies invaded the mainland of Europe one month later, Italy was invaded on 3 September and surrendered on the 8th, the U-boat strength in the Mediterranean had declined to just thirteen boats. Despite their small number the U-boats posed a serious threat to the troop carriers and their supply ships. Indeed *U-617*, *U-565* and *U-410*, as well as *U-593* accounted for Allied ships during September. The latter's contribution was the sinking of the American 7,176 ton ship *William W Gerhard* off the south-west of Italy on the 21st, the torpedoing of another at the same time and the sinking of the small American minesweeper *Skill* on the 25th. On 29 September Italy signed an armistice with the Allies and on 13 October joined them as a 'co-belligerent' in the war against Germany.

On 24 November the Allies made a heavy bombing attack on Toulon, with the U-boat base as the target. Five U-boats were damaged as there were no pens under which the boats could hide.

The Mediterranean U-boats were more than a nuisance value and a plan was put in hand to curtail their actions.

U-boats were forced to operate close to the North African coast, as this was where the convoy routes were. Their manoeuvrability therefore, when escaping from attack, was reduced to half, in comparison with the open ocean conditions in the Atlantic. This reduction made it possible to employ total air saturation with the limited number of anti-U-boat squadrons available in that theatre of operations.

The plan aimed to cover with aircraft the area in which it was anticipated that a U-boat could move after its presence had been established. The U-boat was thus enclosed in a net from which there was no escape. It was eventually exhausted and pounded to destruction by the aircraft or by the surface vessels taking part in the operation.

The plan was code-named Operation Swamp and its intentions were outlined thus:

It aims at covering with aircraft the area in which it is anticipated that a U-boat can move after its presence is known, and is naturally most effective where the enemy is forced to operate against ships proceeding coastwise and within about thirty miles of land.

As soon as a U-boat has disclosed its presence, strike aircraft are despatched to cover a semi-circular area around the position and surface forces are detailed to act as an anti-U-boat striking force to prevent the U-boat from escaping, it is necessary that each part of the area should be swept either visually or by radar at half-hour intervals. As the search continues, the air cover must be spread by increasing the radius of the semi-circle, it being assumed that the U-boat may travel at two knots during the first 24 hours and, thereafter at one knot, as long as it is kept submerged.

The operation is planned in eight hour phases, the area being increased at the end of every eight hours and, as at present designed, calls for 86 flying hours on patrol during the first 24 hours and 144 flying hours on patrol during subsequent periods of 24 hours, when six aircraft will be on patrol at any one time.

That new plans had been prepared to sink U-boats was, of course, unknown to veteran Gerd Kelbling and his crew, survivors of more than a dozen patrols, as they left Marseilles on 1 December. Their patrol area was off the Algerian coast.

At this time the Allies knew that two U-boats were on patrol off North Africa and one off Naples; that one was outward-bound from Pola; that several were in port in Toulon, some damaged by the recent heavy air raid. There was one at Pola and one at Salamis.

In the second week of December Enigma transcripts revealed that four U-boats were operational between Tangier and Bizerta, where an Allied convoy had been sighted.

While *U-593* was still making for the patrol area Kapitänleutnant Karl-Jürg Wächter, in *U-223*, torpedoed HMS *Cuckmere* off the Algerian coast in the early afternoon of 11 December. The frigate was later towed into harbour. At the time of the attack *U-593* was closing near the same area. In fact that night was a very black one and *U-593* felt quite safe in surfacing to recharge its batteries. The anti-aircraft crew were standing by to counter any Leigh light aircraft attacks and T5, homing torpedoes, were loaded in case they should be surprised by a marauding destroyer or escort. One of the U-boat's crew described what happened next:

At 0630 we submerged and the hydrophone operator heard the sound of propellers. The commander immediately took the boat up but there was nothing to be seen. The commander extended the periscope but it was pitch dark. He ordered us to make Tube 2 ready. We confirmed 'Tube 2 ready'. About forty minutes later he ordered the torpedo to be fired. There was an explosion and we heard the ship going down.

Had Gerd Kelbling been able to see the pendant number L96 on the side of the ship he torpedoed, he would immediately have known that he had sunk HMS *Tynedale*, the Hunt class destroyer that had depth-charged him when he was approaching St Nazaire at the end of his first patrol 21 months earlier! Surely one of the most bizarre coincidences of the sea war.

Tynedale had been escorting the eastbound convoy KMS34 and was just north of Djidjelli when attacked. While *U-593* made good its escape in a westerly direction three Wellingtons of No 458 Squadron from Bône were at once ordered to begin Operation Swamp, using *Tynedale*'s position as the datum.

USS *Niblack* and HMS *Holcombe* were detailed to begin hunting immediately, as was HMS *Calpe* later. The latter two, like the victim, were Hunt class destroyers. *Calpe*, launched in the spring of 1941, put to sea not fully manned as many of her crew were ashore in Algiers when the emergency sailing orders arrived.

In the afternoon *U-593*, unaware of the hornets' nest it had stirred up, was some fifteen miles from the position where *Tynedale* had gone down when the sounds of more propellers were heard. They were from HMS *Holcombe* of the hunting force. The U-boat crew could hardly believe their luck when the gnat found its target and the second Hunt class destroyer was sunk in a space of under eight hours. Unfortunately for the U-boat the attack was witnessed, and reported, by an aircraft of 36 Squadron on its way to Bône and Operation Swamp was begun afresh, the position of the second attack now being taken as the centre of the area to be covered. The US ships *Wainwright* and *Benson* were also called into the operation and later surface forces continued the hunt in two groups of two in company.

Just after midnight *U-593* surfaced to recharge its batteries, but was picked up on radar by B-Baker of 36 Squadron. The Wellington homed in to attack. At three-quarters of a mile range the aircraft was hit and again at half-mile. The Wellington lurched to port out of control and the pilot was unable to carry out a depth charge attack. However, the rear gunner opened fire on passing over and silenced the flak from the U-boat. The aircraft's Leigh light had jammed and was not switched on, but *U-593* was identified in the moonlight. The wireless operator sent out a sighting report at 0035 and an SOS, but was able to regain base.

The other two aircraft on patrol at the time, together with HMS *Calpe* proceeded to the U-boat's reported position but it had submerged and was not contacted again. USS *Wainwright* was in a position midway between the North African and Spanish coastline, with *Niblack* and *Benson*, when it was ordered to join *Calpe* to form the hunting group with two in company, at 0120.

Calpe and *Wainwright* teamed up an hour later, probing the deep with their asdic but the evasion Gerd Kelbling carried out was that given in the U-boat commanders' manual:

The objects of the enemy anti-U-boat defence and anti-U-boat hunt are the destruction of the U-boat when discovered either by the immediate use of underwater weapons or by obliging the U-boat to remain submerged up to the extreme limit of endurance, then destroying it as it surfaces. The procedure of the U-boat during an underwater hunt by the enemy must be understood in the main to consist in being active and attempting to escape from the enemy hunt by exploiting every opportunity, instead of remaining passively on the bottom. To be active gives, in all circumstances, the best likelihood of evading the hunt. Procedure when hunted with echo-ranging sets is:

(a) To keep constantly a fine inclination so as to offer the least practicable surface to the action of the echo-ranging set.

(b) To dive to considerable depth and at the same time, by constantly measuring the density and temperature, to determine the best layer, which can be recognised by the weakening of the pulses of the echo-ranging set. The weaker the pulses heard in the U-boat's hydrophones, the smaller and more indistinct the echo returning to the enemy echo-ranging set.

Endeavour:

(a) To make a large turn with little rudder (infrequent zigzagging), then to move off on a straight course to gain distance from the hunt.

(b) To increase speed as the hunt speeds up (or during depth charging), and to stop or proceed at silent speed if the hunt stops. Avoid a high and steady speed, since the loud noise of the propellers in the water like all the other noises can also be picked up by the echo-ranging set.

(c) To open distance in the enemy's wake, if possible, on account of the interference caused in the enemy echo-ranging set.

(d) In narrow waters and close to the coast it is advisable to proceed close under the coast so as to produce between the enemy hunters and the coast distortion of the echo and its dispersion into several echoes.

(e) At distances less than 300 metres from the enemy, search with echo-ranging sets gives no results because, depending on the shortness of the range, absolutely no data, or only inaccurate data, can be obtained.

In fact, while the destroyers were probing, *U-593* managed to surface again for a short while during the night. Doggedly the aircraft searched the surface and the destroyers' asdic operators listened to their sets, awaiting the 'ping' that would indicate they were in touch.

At 0816 *Calpe* had a sound contact, but with no developments. The destroyers persisted at their task through the forenoon watch but it was not until the early afternoon that the next contact was made. The US destroyer picked up a contact and Commander W. W. Strohbehn directed a depth charge attack. At 1412 a five charge pattern was dropped. *Calpe* picked up the contact at 1423 and promptly fired off a ten-pattern charge with a deep setting. As it happened, this turned out to be lethal. *Wainwright* regained contact at 1435 and coached her British team-mate up to the target. *Calpe* despatched another ten-pattern charge at 1440.

What happened in *U-593* when the ten charge pattern was dropped is described by one of the engine room crew below:

We had a pattern of depth charges and tried to dive; then we received a second pattern of depth charges and that was when the inlet valve went. Then we shipped water aft, and it was immediately reported from aft '400 litres of water'. The commander ordered, 'Remain submerged'; everybody rushed forward, nothing happened. We blew No 1 tank, nothing happened. We blew No 3, nothing happened. We shut the emergency escape hatch. We blew No 3 and another tank, nothing happened. The boat was down by the stern again. We still had 30 kilograms of air. The chief electrical mechanic said, 'Sir, we can only blow the tanks once more.'

Commander to Engineering officer:

'Can we still control the boat? Must we give it up?'

The engineering officer really didn't know, but finally said:

'We can't control it any longer.'

'Blow the tanks,' ordered the commander.

HMS *Calpe*

USS *Wainwright*

As we made for the surface the crew went through the practised scuttling procedures, *U-593* was not going to be captured. The fuse was placed aft with the scuttling charges placed forward between the warheads of the torpedoes and set off. The engineering officer was smashing things up in the control room.

As *U-593* broke surface Gerd Kelbling ordered all hands on deck and said, 'Comrades, we shall meet again in captivity.'

The American and British destroyer crews were both surprised and delighted to see *U-593* emerge from a froth of white water. The 'open fire' order was given simultaneously. The British ship opened up with its pom-poms while the American destroyer used its full armaments and at the same time enterprisingly launched a pinnace, hoping to board the U-boat.

Fortunately for the U-boat's crew, the destroyer's ranging shots were off target. The destroyermen had seen the U-boat crew tumbling out and thought they were going to man the guns but they were only getting the rubber dinghy out on the deck and launched it from the bridge. The crew went over the side into the water and began swimming.

Once it was seen that the U-boat crew were abandoning ship and making no attempt to use their guns the destroyers held their fire. Only the commander, engineering officer and one other man were still aboard *U-593*. The commander said: 'We must find some means of making the boat sink more quickly.'

So the torpedo hatch forward was unscrewed and water entered from below. At this moment the American pinnace came alongside and secured to the U-boat. As the Americans scrambled on the foc's'le Gerd Kelbling shouted, 'The torpedoes are going to explode at any moment!' The Americans quickly leapt off, taking the remaining Germans with them. Suddenly the German commander exclaimed, 'Quick, look, she's going!'

The stern of the U-boat came up and then disappeared. There was an explosion and as a large fountain of water gushed up the German crew, who were swimming towards the destroyers, gave a cheer for their old boat. The time was 1508.

The whole crew of 5 officers and 46 men were picked up; only one

U-593 sinking

was wounded slightly. Their average age was found to be in the 20–21 year bracket.

Since the attack on *Tynedale* 32 hours earlier *U-593* had only been able to spend a matter of minutes on the surface. In the same period 21 Wellington sorties had been flown. Operation Swamp, with the co-operation of the air and surface craft, had been a success.

Now for some reaction from the ships' crews. First from a seaman aboard *Wainwright*, the American destroyer that had been launched in 1939:

Most of those anti-U-boat patrols off the North African coast were as boring as a cop's beat in Flatbush, but Murder Inc was out there. You had all the excitement you could handle when you ran into the Germans. Seven minutes after the last depth charge was dropped the U-boat came spouting to the surface a mile away from *Wainwright*. We opened fire, two minutes of this and the crew came running out of the conning tower. Our captain told the gunners to hold their fire and sent a boat away. The destroyermen had time to board the damaged U-boat and bring off men who were calling '*Kamerad*'.

Once aboard the American destroyer the Germans were taken to the boiler room and given the opportunity to clean off the oil they had picked up in the sea. Later Gerd Kelbling met the American captain and his officers. The remaining survivors were picked up by HMS *Calpe*. Scotsman George Auld on the British destroyer remembers:

> My action station in the destroyer was in the TS under the Bridge. When the U-boat came up all the small guns went in to action, pom-poms, oerlikons etc. So we came out to see the show. We collected some of the survivors and when they came on board they were a bit apprehensive. They were stripped and given a towel and a blanket. Needless to say all their clothes were stolen for souvenirs. During the hunt we were just as apprehensive as the Germans. I heard one or two big mouths who said a lot of brave words after it was all over, but I guess many of them had had a laundry problem during the previous night.

At 1530, when all the survivors had been rescued, the two Allied destroyers set course for Algiers.

Under initial interrogation it was established that the U-boat men had a healthy respect for aircraft and had found it impossible to surface for any length of time during the 32-hour period. They had made an attempt at 0030 but had been forced to submerge because of the Wellington attack. Although not injured they appeared to be considerably exhausted and unnerved by their experiences. They had been short of air and their commander had instructed them to move about as little as possible. Their batteries were running low and they were unable to take violent evading action against *Calpe*'s and *Wainwright*'s depth charge attacks.

Operation Swamp had proved itself successful and in the next few days there were opportunities to consolidate the plan.

CHAPTER SEVEN

Eagle Avenged

In August 1942 the main task of the Mediterranean Fleet was to supply the beleaguered island of Malta with aircraft, ammunition and food supplies. In June, out of a double pronged convoy from Port Said and Gibraltar, only two merchantmen from Gibraltar arrived and the Port Said convoy was forced to turn back. The island, which had been awarded the George Cross by King George VI earlier in the year, was getting desperate; food supplies were extremely short and fuel oil for the defending ships and aircraft was running dangerously low.

A last vital attempt to relieve the island fortress was launched: Operation Pedestal, a force of fourteen merchant ships with the heaviest escort that could be supplied, set out to relieve the island. Four aircraft carriers were included in the force.

The Germans and Italians intent on maintaining their stranglehold, were alerted and ready to meet this last-ditch attempt at relief; they let fly with their shore-based aircraft on an unprecedented scale, operating at short range from Sardinia and Sicily. They set up a U-boat trap deploying their boats in a triple line of attack. Five Italian and two German U-boats were ordered to first locate, and then to attack the convoy, special targets were specified as the aircraft-carriers. The German boats were *U-73* and *U-205*. Strangely the latter had also taken second place in the sinking of the carrier *Ark Royal* nine months earlier.

In the early afternoon of 11 August the ships' crews were tensed and ready for the first sight of Axis aircraft, but it was from beneath the waves that the first serious attack materialised. The veteran aircraft carrier HMS *Eagle* of 22,600 tons was stationed well over on the starboard quarter of the convoy, steaming at thirteen knots, on

127

the starboard leg of a zigzag. She had a four aircraft patrol of Sea Hurricanes aloft at the time, who were sharing this duty with four from the *Victorious*. At 1315 observers saw four explosions along her port side and she immediately began to list to port. In fact the first torpedo had struck the carrier's port quarter and was followed in ten seconds by three more. After the first hit *Eagle* heeled five degrees to port and this increased to fifteen degrees after the final hit. All the explosions occurred in the vicinity of the port side engine room; no immediate damage was caused in the centre or starboard engine-rooms. A, C and D boiler rooms in the centre flooded and in each case the port wing bulkhead collapsed. She finally settled bodily at thirty degrees and sank within eight minutes.

It was the experienced Kapitänleutnant Helmut Rosenbaum, operating out of Spezia in *U-73*, who had carried out the attack. He had detected the approach of the convoy by the sound of advancing propeller noises and had at once come up to periscope depth and made his approach. A quarter of an hour later the masts of a destroyer approaching were sighted and at the same time Rosenbaum caught sight of a carrier. He estimated the speed of the carrier at twelve knots, she was zigzagging with six escorts around her as she passed the U-boat some four miles away. Cursing his misfortune Rosenbaum continued his course.

An hour passed, then another destroyer came up at high speed, passed close by *U-73*'s position and continued in the direction taken by the carrier group. When almost out of sight she started signalling and then returned the way she had come, again passing almost over the U-boat without detecting it.

The U-boat commander waited until she had passed and then took another look through the periscope and at once sighted the convoy approaching him from the west. He counted eight freighters, a battleship, two cruisers and eight destroyers. Now was the time that all the things learned in training and from experience were brought to bear; this was the culmination of a U-boat commander's dreams, an enemy fleet approaching and he was undetected. Working up to full speed Rosenbaum closed the target and identified a carrier as the last ship in the starboard line.

Rosenbaum counted seven destroyers between him and his target, which he correctly identified as *Eagle*. Undisturbed by the fact that his boat was operating at less than full efficiency – defects included an unserviceable direction-finding aerial, a leaking exhaust cut-out, leaks in the bilge pump and periscope – he at once went into the attack making a text-book approach on the carrier. He closed, undetected by the destroyer screen, to within five hundred yards of the carrier before firing a full salvo of four torpedoes from the bow tubes.

In making its approach the U-boat had passed between two destroyers with under four hundred yards to spare on either side. After the attack *U-73* dived deeply, flooding the bow tanks with all spare hands crowded for'ard as four explosions were heard and twelve minutes later the roar of the carrier's boilers blowing under water shook the submerged boat. Only then did the first depth-charges arrive.

For about an hour-and-a-half after the sinking numerous sightings of U-boats and torpedoes and asdic contacts were reported. Meanwhile *U-73* had crept away at 500 feet, its hull creaking frighteningly at such unaccustomed pressures. All the auxiliary machinery was stopped and the bilge-pump stationary, with water leaking in through the defective cut-out and periscope. For three hours the commander stayed at this depth but no further depth-charges arrived so the U-boat was brought carefully to the surface. Oil leaking from the hull was mingled with that from the sunken carrier, successfully hiding its whereabouts. Rosenbaum signalled to Admiral Kreisch, C-in-C in the Mediterranean, the composition speed and bearing of the convoy, adding that he had sunk *Eagle*. At 2200 the Deutscher Rundfunk broadcast a special news bulletin; Rosenbaum was awarded the Knight's Cross of the Iron Cross for this brilliant attack.

It was a glorious way for Kapitänleutnant Helmut Rosenbaum to finish his eighteen-month reign as commander of *U-73*. On arrival back at La Spezia he and his crew were fêted and later he was appointed to a shore posting.

So ended a fruitful partnership that began back at the end of July 1940, when the Type VIIB boat was launched from the Bremer Vulkan yard at Vegesack. Helmut Rosenbaum was appointed commander and a young officer, Horst Deckert, who had been born in Egypt of German-American parents, was chosen to be his 2WO.

At this stage of the war England was on her own, Germany was in command of all the European mainland; most of France was occupied, so after leaving Heligoland for its first operation on 8 February 1941, *U-73* was detailed to put in to Lorient. On this initial patrol *U-73* bagged its first victim when the 4,260 ton British ship *Waynegate* was torpedoed while sailing in a convoy outward bound from Liverpool to North America. The steamer was one of nine ships in convoy OB288 sunk by U-boats that night. In its first wolf pack attack *U-73* had notched up a success. Four days later *U-73* was safely escorted into Lorient. These were the days of celebrations, with flowers and bands, when a U-boat reached port. The U-boat remained at the 10th Flotilla base for four weeks before commencing its next patrol, to the North Atlantic.

A pack of U-boats were awaiting convoy SC26 of fully laden ships sailing from Nova Scotia to Britain. Six ships of the, then unescorted, convoy were sunk and *U-73* was in part responsible for three of them. First the 5,724 ton British steamer *Westpool* was sunk at 0410 on 3 April and 25 minutes later the 6,895 ton ship *British Viscount* was also torpedoed and sunk. After remaining submerged throughout the day, *U-73* surfaced in the evening when the 5,351 ton British ship *Athenic* was seen through the periscope. The ship had been torpedoed earlier in the day by Endrass in *U-46* but did not sink, so *U-73* delivered the *coup de grâce*.

The next success did not come until Hitler's birthday, seventeen days later, and this was a three-in-one sinking. In darkness, during the early hours, *U-73* torpedoed the British 8,570 ton steamer *Empire Endurance* which was carrying two motor launches, *ML 1003* and *ML 1037*, as deck cargo. Three days later *U-73* returned to Lorient claiming over 26,000 tons of shipping sunk on the patrol.

After leave *U-73* left Lorient, on 20 May, for the last time, bound for the North Atlantic again. Bad luck dogged the patrol. In broad daylight on 4 June the commander attacked a 7,000 ton ship; watching through the periscope he saw a torpedo hit the ship, but it did not explode.

After a month at sea *U-73* returned to France, this time to the base at St Nazaire, where it came under the control of the 6th Flotilla. While serving with the new flotilla the partnership was not at all productive. After leaving for patrol on 29 June *U-73* had to return five days later with an engine defect. The next two patrols produced no successes.

When wished 'A Happy New Year' Helmut Rosenbaum could not have visualised what 1942 held in store for him. He was under orders to sail for the Mediterranean, and warmer climes, on 3 January and passed through the Straits of Gibraltar on the night of the 13/14th of the month.

The first Mediterranean patrol, under the command of the 29th Flotilla, was off the North African coast, here, just before midnight on 3 February, an attack was carried out on a destroyer. Two detonations were heard but no ship was reported sunk.

Although, like all the other Mediterranean boats, *U-73* was kept very busy, it was not until August that it had its greatest success, in sinking the aircraft carrier *Eagle*, thus ending the career of this fine old ship that had played such a vital part in the supplying of Malta, in just eight minutes, the time it took her to sink.

Kapitänleutnant Helmut Rosenbaum was succeeded as commander of *U-73* by Horst Deckert, who at the beginning of the commission had been 2WO of the boat. A product of the first 1937 class for Kriegsmarine officers, he had progressed from 2WO to 1WO, had then taken his commanding officer's course, on the recommendation of Helmut Rosenbaum, and now he was to follow his illustrious former commander, in command. The crew were pleased at the continuity, 'better the devil you know'.

This Egyptian-born, German-educated U-boat commander must surely have been the only one serving whose parents were living in America, in Chicago to be exact!

The first success for the new commander came six days after the Allies had landed in North Africa; 14 November, east of Gibraltar. A 6,000 ton ship was attacked, the torpedo was seen to hit and later twenty survivors were seen in the water. On New Year's Day there was an attack taken straight from the text book of U-boat commanders' instructions:

The classical attack from the stern tubes is only carried out when the U-boat is ahead of the enemy, or else when, owing to an unexpected alteration of course on the part of the enemy, it turns out to be more advantageous to fire from stern tubes than from bow tubes. If the U-boat is ahead of the enemy it must steer towards him for a stern shot; steering towards him is more advantageous than allowing itself to be overtaken by the enemy, because when it has to turn on to the attacking course it makes a turn smaller by two director angles than in the opposite case. Do not turn too soon, or the range of firing will be too great. *Keep a good hold on your nerves.*

In mid-afternoon, off the North African coast near Oran, the American 7,176 ton ship *Arthur Middleton* was at a range of only 250 metres when the stern tube was fired. Just seventeen seconds later the ship exploded as the torpedo struck home. Two days later, in the same area, another attack was made, two detonations were heard, but the Allies lost no ships on this day.

At some time during this period *U-73* landed French-speaking spies off Oran. The crew were not told anything about their passengers and the commander was acting under sealed orders.

Towards the end of March *U-77* was sunk by aircraft from Nos 233 and 48 Squadrons in the western Mediterranean. At the time *U-73* was quite close and one of the crew reported:

Our boat got a hell of a battering too. The boat was badly damaged; a bomb went through the torpedo hatch at a depth of 42 metres. The pressure hull and everything was smashed. The torpedo hatch was stove in. We surfaced and managed to reach base, where the pressure hull was repaired.

By now the Allies had cleared the Axis forces from North Africa and their next objective was Sicily, before attacking the mainland of Italy. The build up of shipping for the forthcoming invasion meant plenty of targets for the hard-pressed U-boats.

On 21 June the small British boat *Brinkburn* was torpedoed and sunk by *U-73* and six days later a most desirable target, the 8,300 ton Royal Fleet Auxiliary *Abbeydale* was seen through the periscope. This tanker had been replenishing the Mediterranean fleet at sea. The RFA was torpedoed, but did not sink; nevertheless, this was a blow for the Allies.

The next target for *U-73* was the American cruiser USS

Philadelphia. Three months earlier the cruiser had collided with a destroyer, putting both ships out of action temporarily. Now, on 11 August, while assisting in the invasion of Sicily it was sighted by *U-73*. In the evening the U-boat fired at the cruiser, heard two hits and assumed it had sunk; it hadn't. This was the thirteenth war patrol of the U-boat, the superstitious crew members were apprehensive when told the American cruiser was their target. They need not have worried, for they escaped without a depth charge being dropped or even an aircraft search. This was in direct contrast to another occasion when they remained submerged for forty hours. The chief engineer and some of his ratings were poisoned and the remainder of the crew had pains in their chests and ached all over.

On 18 October *U-73* attacked a 6,000 ton freighter fifty miles west of Algiers; it was claimed sunk, but in fact it wasn't even hit. The next proper success came just after midnight on 3 November when the French 4,581 ton steamer *Mont Viso* was torpedoed and sunk.

The successful U-boat, that had far exceeded the eighty day expectation for survival, commenced its fifteenth, and last patrol on 3 December. For Kapitänleutnant Horst Deckert it was his sixth patrol in command, and his charge was one of only thirteen U-boats still on operations in the Mediterranean. As has been seen earlier the Allies were stepping up pressure with sustained anti-U-boat saturation hunting techniques.

An eight-and-a-half knot convoy, of 24 ships with escorts, left Alexandria, dropped some ships off at Bône and picked up others from the Algerian port. Among the US bound ships was the American 7,176 ton tanker *John S Copley*. On 16 December this tanker was the target singled out for attention by Horst Deckert. The ship was hit by a triple fan salvo from *U-73*; she listed to port but did not sink. Two lifeboats were seen to leave the tanker, which later made harbour.

Hunting *U-73* were HMS *Brilliant* and US destroyers *Edison*, *Trippe* and *Woolsey*. The Americans sailed out of Mers-el-Kebir to track down *U-73*. *Edison* was detailed to assist in the screening and to pick up survivors from the tanker. The force reached the area in the late afternoon and started an anti-U-boat search. Within 45 minutes *Woolsey* picked up a contact. As the others in the force closed the contact evaporated so the hunters held their depth charges, waiting for a sharper materialisation of the target. This came just after 1830, *Woolsey* regained a sound contact and the attack commenced. What happened is best described by one of the U-boat's crew:

> About midday we attacked an 8,000 ton ship, a corvette and a transport. I don't know whether they were sunk. One hunter after another came after us all afternoon. We were at 20 metres the whole time, we didn't go any deeper, but none of them dropped depth charges.
>
> At about 1830 another one joined, and *Crash!* They dropped depth charges on us. They landed right under the boat and immediately there was an inrush of water for'ard, by the torpedo compartment; water from the diesel got into the electric motors and the air was almost all used up – we had to keep blowing the tanks. We had plunged to 160 metres, then up again and down again and up again. We had to surface. It was dark, there was nothing to be seen.
>
> 'Three-quarter speed ahead,' ordered the commander – the diesels were still working. Suddenly there was a shout from all sides, they had got us amidships. Then the firing really began. Everybody got out of the boat, but some drowned as there was quite a heavy sea.

Woolsey's radar picked up the now surfaced and damaged *U-73* at a range of over a mile. *Woolsey* and *Trippe* shot the ray of a powerful searchlight across the sea. As the beams fastened on to the U-boat, the German gunners opened fire. *Woolsey* was the target and hot steel whistled across the deck and two ratings were wounded. The destroyers returned the fire and *U-73* was lashed into sinking wreckage. USS *Trippe* and *Woolsey* were credited with sinking *U-73* 25 miles north-west of Oran, seventeen months after *Eagle* had been sunk in the same sea. The aircraft carrier had been avenged. Kapitänleutnant Horst Deckert and 33 members of his successful U-boat's crew were plucked from the water and taken prisoner. One of them had a superstitious little tale to relate:

> On our 13th patrol, 13 is our lucky number, we sank a cruiser

(USS *Philadelphia*) and we didn't get a single depth charge during that whole patrol and also no air attacks. Then on this last patrol, our 15th, we had bad luck on 13 December when our four barrel gun was destroyed. On the 13th day of the patrol we were sunk and taken prisoner.

CHAPTER EIGHT

Year's End

The already recorded sinking of *U-645* on Christmas Eve signalled the end of the 1943 hunting season in which 237 U-boats were lost. A breakdown of the figures shows that 148 were lost to the Royal Navy and Coastal Command, 75 to American forces, five to the French and one to the Russians. The remaining eight were lost as a result of collisions or accidents.

Four accidents had occurred in the last five weeks. On 18 November the Type VIIC *U-718*, built in Hamburg by Stülcken Sohn and launched at the end of March, sank. The boat had commissioned on 25 June with Oberleutnant Helmut Wieduwildt in command and while still working up was lost in the West Baltic by an accidental collision with *U-476*.

Two days later U-boat headquarters were alarmed to learn that another boat was lost in the same area. This time it was a Wilhelmshaven built Type VIIC boat. After being launched from the Naval dockyard *U-768* had been commissioned under Oberleutnant Johann Buttjer on 14 October. Again, while training in the West Baltic, the U-boat was sunk in an accidental collision with *U-745*.

In the middle of December yet another U-boat that had not had time to join the sea war was lost. General Arnold of the USAAF declared:

> The Allies are almost ready to launch a 24-hour 360-degree bombing assault on Germany from North, South, East and West. We are going to hit them every day and the RAF every night.

On Saturday, 11 December, the sirens in the Emden area sounded as the Eighth Air Force carried out a heavy raid on the U-boat yards. Much damage was caused but the Americans lost twenty aircraft in the raid. Undeterred they carried out a similar raid on Kiel two days later. In this raid *U-345*, a Type VIIC boat commissioned at Emden in mid-April, was badly damaged. German records say the boat 'was salvaged and paid off ten days later, thus not becoming operational.'

The crew of *U-284*, on their first patrol, encountered enough action to last them a lifetime. The Type VIIC boat, built by Bremer Vulkan and launched from Vegesack at the beginning of March, was commissioned by Oberleutnant Gunter Scholz. After training in the Baltic the boat left Kiel-Wik on its first patrol, to the North Atlantic, on 23 November. When in a position 480 miles south-east of Greenland on 21 December the boat was so badly storm damaged that it had to be scuttled. The crew were picked up by *U-629* out from Bergen on its fourth patrol. U-boat headquarters sent instructions to Oberleutnant Hans-Helmut Bugs commanding the rescue boat, to return the survivors immediately. His overcrowded boat was well into the Bay of Biscay, and less than 24 hours from safety, when it was picked up on the radar of an aircraft flying 800 feet above in the early hours of 4 January.

The Wellington of No 304 Polish Squadron was on an anti-U-boat patrol in the Bay of Biscay when the radar indicated a contact at seven miles. The aircraft homed immediately and at three-quarters of a mile the pilot sighted a long white wake, and immediately afterwards a surfaced U-boat, heading on a north-easterly course, which was making the wake. As *U-629* was fully visible, the pilot decided not to switch on the Leigh light. He turned his aircraft slightly to starboard and attacked from the port quarter. Six Torpex depth charges were released, spaced at sixty feet, and these were seen to straddle the U-boat. The rear gunner raked *U-629*'s deck with bullets and many hits were seen. After the depth charges exploded there was a big flash of light on the deck. The U-boat was seen to have slowed and was lost to view as the radar contact disappeared when *U-629* submerged. Fortunately for the Germans, the sturdy overloaded U-boat survived this attack and the next day nearly one hundred men tumbled out of the conning tower when *U-629* reached Brest.

Vickers Wellingtons of No 304 Squadron

Eight days before *U-284* had sunk the crew of another boat on its first patrol were not so fortunate, for their boat, *U-391*, was the last one to be lost in the Bay of Biscay in 1943. The U-boat, a Type VIIC, was built at the Howaldtz Werke at Kiel and launched on 5 March 1943. The shipbuilders at Kiel were fortunate that at this time the Ruhr, Berlin, Wilhelmshaven and the U-boat bases at Lorient and St Nazaire were the recipients of RAF night bombing raids and so they had a temporary respite.

Oberleutnant Gert Dültgen was appointed to command the new U-boat. After its preliminary working up in the Baltic the U-boat left its home town of Kiel on 2 October. It probably put in at a Norwegian base before setting out on its first war patrol, joining with a pack of U-boats seeking convoys between Sierra Leone and Gibraltar to the United Kingdom. As earlier recorded *U-391* was one of a second line of U-boats waiting to intercept convoy SL139/MKS30 on 20 November. It did not make contact with the merchant ships or even the escort.

On the evening of 12 December, having completed its patrol,

U-391 was north-west of Cape Ortegal, making its way into the Bay of Biscay prior to entering its new French base.

At 2250 Liberator R-Rodger of 53 Squadron, flying an anti-U-boat patrol over the Bay, picked up a radar contact, closed the position and its Leigh light illuminated a U-boat submerging, before the pilot, Flight Lieutenant J. Burton, could get into a position to attack. A sighting report was transmitted to base and R-Rodger resumed patrol.

Another 53 Squadron Liberator, B-Baker, took off from Beaulieu at 0015. The pilot, Squadron Leader G. Crawford, had been airborne for half-an-hour when he received a message from base ordering him to search in the vicinity of the position where the other aircraft had sighted the U-boat. This position was reached at 0413 and a square search was commenced. The Mark V radar became partially unserviceable and the pilot ordered that it should be used only for periods of three minutes at three-minute intervals. It was considered that but for this action the radar would soon have ceased to work at all. As the square search was proving to be unproductive the pilot returned to the first position and began again. There was six-tenths light strato-cumulus cloud and visibility was two miles up moon and less than a quarter-of-a-mile down moon. At 0656, while the Liberator was flying at 1,500 feet, a radar contact was obtained on the port quarter at a range of seven-and-a-half miles. The aircraft turned to home but during approach radar and the intercom temporarily failed. As a result, when the Leigh light was switched on the U-boat was not illuminated, but it immediately opened fire. Flak bursts hit the Liberator which was betraying its position with its light. The fire was accurate and concentrated from a position about 1,300 yards away on the starboard beam. The U-boat, *U-391*, was on a westerly course and was zig-zagging violently at fifteen knots. The Liberator's Leigh light and radar were switched off, but as it turned away to port the aircraft was silhouetted against the moon and the German gunners scored more hits. The aircraft circled to port and lost contact for a few minutes until *U-391* again opened fire.

In carrying out his ack-ack attacks the new commander in his new U-boat was carrying out to the letter the instructions laid down in the U-boat commanders' manual:

On the approach of aircraft at night and in a calm sea, reduce speed until the tell-tale white wake disappears. If at night an aircraft is sighted at short range when the U-boat is actually heading towards it, do not submerge; defend yourself with machine-gun fire. It is more dangerous to be hit by bombs during the submerging manoeuvre than when surfaced. The danger of being sighted and attacked by aircraft on clear moonlight nights is great. In specially dangerous areas, therefore, post a fifth lookout, to act also as a machine-gunner standing by the ready-loaded machine-guns.

Although carrying out the text book instructions the U-boat, however, soon lost touch and ceased fire, probably the aerial could not pick up the aircraft's radar signal if it was switched off at the time. The Liberator was able to manoeuvre into position for an up-moon attack. The aircraft came in just forward of the U-boat's beam and, with the help of the Mark III bomb sight, dropped six depth charges from 130 feet. Neither the radar nor the Leigh light was used during the run-in, which was straight and level. The air-gunners, by their captain's orders, held their fire in order not to reveal the aircraft's position. At 300 yards the Germans opened fire without scoring any hits and the front gunner immediately replied spraying the conning tower and tracer hit the superstructure in a steady stream. The rear gunner stated that the depth charges straddled the conning tower and that he saw two explosions.

The Liberator turned to port and when on a reciprocal course a very small sharp radar contact was obtained a mile-and-a-quarter abaft the port beam. The aircraft set course for the position, but the blip disappeared almost at once. It is thought that this blip may have been caused by the bow or stern of the U-boat for, when the Liberator passed over the position, the crew saw a flame float which they had dropped at the time of the attack. After about a quarter-of-an-hour what appeared to be a flashing light was seen in the water, but it disappeared before it could be found. A second flashing light later turned out to be a flame float. The Liberator then made a number of runs over the position, using the Leigh light. During the first run the pilot, navigator and front gunner saw two bodies in the water, one with his head and shoulders showing as though he was

HMS *HURRICANE*

HMS *DUKE OF YORK*

wearing a life-jacket. On the third run, at a hundred feet, both the navigator and the front gunner saw a body and what appeared to be a survivor. Shortly after this a Halifax and Sunderland arrived and the pilot of Liberator set course for base.

Squadron Leader Crawford, the pilot, who had joined the squadron less than a month before, was feeling elated but weary as he approached the English coast. He was less than pleased when his wireless operator told him that due to bad weather conditions at base their Liberator, B2814, was to land at Davidson Moor. Given a new course by the navigator the pilot drew on his last reserves of energy as he thankfully let down the nose and main wheels and landed his damaged Liberator safely at the unfamiliar airfield. It was 1350; the Liberator and its crew had spent thirteen hours and thirty-five minutes in the air.

An official summing up of the attack concluded: 'The complete operation reflects great credit on the whole crew.'

The U-boat had notified base that it was being attacked but the worst was not known until *U-391* failed to respond to later signals. No survivors were rescued.

The demise of *U-391* concludes the story of U-boat losses for 1943, the last of which was *U-645* on Christmas Eve. There were no more U-boat losses for fifteen days, as if in fact Britain had declared an amnesty over Christmas and the New Year. However, there was no closed season in the U-boat and surface fleet war.

As already related *U-645* had been sunk by USS *Schenck* screening the carrier *Card*, but it was by no means a one sided contest as USS *Leary* was sunk by *U-275* and HMS *Hurricane* by *U-415*. That Christmas Eve Friday of 1943 will never be forgotten by John W. Kennedy, serving in the destroyer *Hurricane*:

I joined the Navy as a boy earlier in the year, the *Hurricane* being my first ship, and was torpedoed after only three weeks on board. My rank was a signalman. My recollections are that the torpedo struck *Hurricane* at two minutes past seven in the evening. We managed to keep afloat during the night but had to transfer on Christmas Day morning to the frigate *Glenarm*. My last job on the destroyer was to hoist battle ensigns at each yardarm before the ship went down.

It was initially thought that *Hurricane* could be saved. At 2240 she reported that she 'was in no danger of sinking but was unable to steer'. When the survivors had been transferred to other ships HMS *Hurricane* was sunk by British forces.

On the fringe of the U-boat war the Allies, through codebreaking, knew that five blockade runners were expected at the Biscay coast and U-boats often signalled sightings of them. These ships carried vital supplies such as rubber from the Far East. *Osorno* reached the Gironde safely, but this was the only ship to do so. *Alsterufer*, of which more later, was sunk on Boxing Day. *Regensburg* and the others were sunk in the South Atlantic by American forces.

Also lost on Boxing Day was *Scharnhorst* and U-boats were told to look for survivors. The German battleship had hoped to annihilate an Arctic convoy but Admiral Sir Bruce Frazer, Commander-in-Chief Home Fleet, flying his flag in HMS *Duke of York*, with a force of cruisers and destroyers, was waiting for just such a move. *Scharnhorst* became separated from her accompanying destroyers and when finally caught took heavy punishment before sinking in flames in what has become known as The Battle of North Cape.

So ended 1943, a year in which 597 Allied and neutral ships had been sunk.

CHAPTER NINE

Lull before the Storm

At the beginning of 1944 there were 30 U-boats at sea in the North Atlantic. Ten were well out to sea and the others, in small groups, were in the area between the west of Ireland and to the south of Iceland. Instead of remaining in one position, these groups of two or three boats kept constantly on the move, changing their relative position and opening out and closing in, so as to prevent the Allies from establishing the exact extent of their disposition. At the end of 1943 this bought some success as several convoys were intercepted, but conversely having only a small number of U-boats available the object of sinking the convoys could not be achieved with such a small attacking force. Thus the argument in favour of disposition of small groups was disproved.

While the U-boats were not attacking they were also not being sunk; a fortnight had elapsed since a U-boat was sunk.

On 7 January the groups were dispersed and the U-boats allocated, singly, to attack areas west of the British Isles. This step signalled the abandonment of the patrol line and scouting formations for convoy interception, except when air reconnaissance was available. The fact that the virtual discontinuance of pack attacks would further diminish the prospect of successes was accepted and henceforth independent U-boats had generally to cope single-handed with the entire convoy escort and bear the brunt of the counter attacks.

The first U-boat to suffer from these new allocations was *U-757*, a Type VIIC boat that had been active for fifteen months but had not caused the Allies too much inconvenience. The boat was built in the naval dockyard at Wilhelmshaven and Kapitänleutnant Friedrich Deetz was appointed in command. The initial, three-day, patrol took the U-boat from Kiel, on 15 September 1942, up through the Kattegat and Skagerrak to Bergen. After eight days in the Norwegian port *U-757* set out on its first, month-long, war patrol to the North Atlantic. The U-boat returned to St Nazaire on 24 October with no successes to report. After seven weeks at base the second patrol, to the North Atlantic, started on 12 December but the boat returned two weeks later, on Christmas Day – something was wrong. It was two months before *U-757* was cleared to put to sea again and on 22 February Kapitänleutnant Deetz sailed on his third patrol. The North Atlantic was again the chosen area and hopes were high, there were plenty of U-boats and convoys at sea. In the evening of 28 February, to the west of the Bay of Biscay, a large ship was attacked and a possible hit by a FAT was reported. The next attack, and the first successful one came in the early hours of 11 March. A total of thirteen U-boats formed round the heavily escorted homeward-bound convoy HX228. Included in the pack with *U-757* were *U-86*, *U-496*, *U-444*, *U-336*, *U-221*, *U-228*, *U-359*, *U-432*, *U-440*, *U-590*. Oberleutnant Albert Langfeld in *U-444* torpedoed a 7,000 ton steamer and was then rammed and sunk by *Harvester*, the senior officer of the escort. In turn *Harvester*, so damaged by the ramming, was sunk by *U-432*. At 0325 on the 11th *U-757* hit the 5,000 ton Norwegian munition ship *Brant County* which immediately exploded and in doing so severely damaged the U-boat. Just over an hour later *U-757* delivered the *coup de grâce* to *William C. Gorgas*, the 7,000 ton steamer that had been torpedoed by *U-444* earlier. The U-boat had opened its account and a relieved commander, in a damaged boat, set course for base which was reached a week later. The U-boat had made its contribution to the sinking of 108 Allied ships in March. It was nearly four months before *U-757* was fit to return to sea and therefore it missed the Atlantic battles in May which cost the U-boat arm dearly.

A new patrol zone was assigned for the fourth war patrol, the area off West Africa and *U-757* set out for these warmer climes on 7 July. Exactly a month later, off the coast of Sierra Leone, *U-757* intercepted, torpedoed and sank the 4,000 ton Norwegian motorship *Fernhill*. This was the only success of the patrol to be reported when the U-boat returned to St Nazaire on 4 September. Once more the crew spent some time ashore, not setting off again until after

HMS *BAYNTUN* . . .
. . . and the Officers and Petty Officers

Christmas. On 29 December *U-757* left base for the last time. New Year's Eve saw it making for its patrol area to the south-west of Ireland.

While the German submariners were celebrating a hull full of fresh air after charging their batteries, two members of the Captain class frigate HMS *Bayntun* were also celebrating, but in a different way, ashore at Londonderry. One, Petty Officer Jim Creasey, a veteran of the Malta convoys, was captain of the quarterdeck and at action stations was in charge of the after twin 4in guns. Another of his duties was to look after the 'foxer' or rattling gear. This consisted, on *Bayntun*, of two iron bars about 3-4 feet long in a small frame. When the frigate was travelling at speed and not 'pinging' for U-boats two were towed well astern of the ship. The force of the sea caused them to bang together and this, making a greater noise than the ship's screws, acted as a counter measure attracting acoustic torpedoes to it rather than to the ship.

HMS *Bayntun*, frigate pendant number K310, had been commissioned in America early in 1943 and the British sailors were astonished to find a laundry, showers and an ice cream bar installed. The new frigates supplemented the close escorts of convoys, moving from one convoy to another during their six-week tours of duty at sea. At the beginning of 1944 there were 23 in operation in the North Atlantic.

The second *Bayntun* crew member to welcome in the New Year was stoker Stan Lawrence. He had just joined the ship and was apprehensive about his first trip to sea in one of HM ships.

The escort group sailed from Moville, out through Lough Foyle, at 2100 on 4 January. A full complement of 160 depth charges was carried aboard *Bayntun* as the escort caught up with convoy OS64/KMS38, bound for Sierra Leone and the Mediterranean area.

On the 6th *U-757* signalled in to U-boat headquarters a sighting, possibly the convoy or its escorts. Stan Lawrence, the 'green' stoker, takes up the story:

We proceeded south down the west coast of Ireland, the weather was as you would expect for that time of the year, with something like a Force 6 wind blowing. We had quite a few false asdic pings.

On Friday 7 January I came off the first dog watch, which I had spent in the after engine room, and, almost immediately 'Action Stations' sounded. I rushed to join my post with the damage control party.

At the time of the action stations sounding at 1805 *Bayntun* was on the extended screen on the port bow of the convoy 330 miles south-west of Cape Clear. An asdic sighting had been confirmed and *Bayntun* heavily attacked the target. The first attack, at 1849, probably did not cause any damage to the U-boat, *U-757*. A second attack, by the Canadian Flower class corvette HMCS *Camrose*, which had now joined, was considered to be a fairly accurate attack – this was an hour after *Bayntun*'s first attack. Some twenty minutes later *Bayntun* attacked again and although possibly the depth charge settings may have been adjusted to explode too deep the charges must have damaged the U-boat as oil was seen shortly afterwards. *Camrose* then made two more attacks. After the first an air bubble came to the surface and indicated that Friedrich Deetz was endeavouring to alter the trim of *U-757* by flooding the tanks and releasing the air outboard. It was encouragement for the hunters above. The fourth attack, by *Camrose*, was considered to have been a good one and oil and wreckage appeared. At this time the captain of *Bayntun* was careful not to get in the way of the Canadian ship.

Camrose came in for a fifth attack at 2130 and thirteen minutes later *Bayntun* carried out its third attack. These attacks were made after 'HE noises' were heard on the bearing. These were the last noises ever heard from *U-757*. Although the search continued into the early hours of 8 January, which is the date given for the sinking, it is almost certain that the earlier attack when wreckage and wood splinters were observed must have been mortal.

The stoker concludes his recollections:

We made about three depth charge runs and were told that a large amount of oil had come up along with a cushion, and the captain thought it was a kill. This was not confirmed until about a week later and I believe we did splice the mainbrace and before arriving at Gibraltar we had it painted on the funnel.

I think my real feelings after it was over were of dis-

U-426 sinking

appointment, I was nearly nineteen but had gone through the London blitz and seen the Battle of Britain with all the involvement.

Petty Officer Jim Creasey says:

> On this attack, or on any of them, I don't think our guns crew were scared, we were experienced and always confident of success. In the past when dropping patterns of depth charges sometimes we would blow up a shoal of fish. Being prepared in case this happened we had nets fixed to a wire loop attached to a bearing out spar. The captain would ease speed for a short while so we could net some. Then the chef would cook the fresh fish for supper.

In the darkness, and the danger of the attack, no fish were landed on that night, the night when the first U-boat of 1944 was sunk. There were no survivors from the boat that had once been part of a wolf pack.

While the crews of *Bayntun* and *Camrose* were awaiting confirmation of their sinking a Coastal Command aircrew had no such worries with the second U-boat to be sunk in 1944.

The victim was Oberleutnant Christian Reich and his crew aboard the Type VIIC boat *U-426*. Built at the Danziger Werft, the boat was a new one and had only been launched eleven months previously. After successfully completing all its trials *U-426* left Kiel on 14 September and spent three days sailing through the Kattegat and Skagerrak up to Bergen. This counted as an initial cruise. The first war cruise commenced eighteen days later when *U-426* was ordered from the Norwegian port to carry out a North Atlantic patrol in search of convoys for a pack attack and on completion to return to Brest which would be its new base.

A fifty-two ship convoy, ONS20, had assembled off the northern end of the Irish sea and sailed on the morning of 10 October. The convoy was escorted by the 4th Escort Group comprising seven Captain-class frigates. U-boat headquarters knew of the convoy and directed U-boats to intercept, what the headquarters did not know was that a faster convoy had left two days later and was only fifteen miles apart from it on 18th, well out to sea. The Germans thought

Short Sunderland of No 10 RAAF Squadron

that the second convoy was a decoy group; this information was monitored by the Admiralty and consequently the escort, Group B7, was switched from the fast convoy to join the more vulnerable slower convoy. Two boats, *U-470* and *U-631*, had been lost in the vicinity of the convoys and only *U-309* and *U-426* claimed to have attacked either convoy.

The one success against the convoy was achieved by *U-426* when, in the darkness in the late evening of 15 October, the British 6,625 ton steamer *Essex Lance*, which was lagging two miles astern of the convoy, was torpedoed and sunk. She broke in half and was abandoned but the entire crew were taken off by the convoy's rescue ship. Later *U-842* signalled in that it had seen some of her empty lifeboats, thus confirming to U-boat headquarters the name of the victim.

By the time the two convoys had crossed the Atlantic six U-boats had been sunk round them. The only success had been achieved by *U-426* and the crew were satisfied with their Danzig-built boat; it had brought them success and taken them back to a French port. The Danzig boats were not usually popular with their crews. The only other boat to fire at the convoy, *U-309*, fired a four torpedo spread on the 17th but no hits were made.

In the four weeks before 5 October, when *U-426* left Bergen, eight U-boats that had left Norwegian bases on their first patrol did not survive them.

The successful U-boat entered Brest on 29 November. Being a new boat it was equipped with Naxos, which detected short-wave radar transmissions, and the updated anti-aircraft armament. These appurtenances gave U-boat control enough confidence for Admiral Dönitz to give permission for boats fitted with them to surface by day when crossing the Bay of Biscay if necessary. For *U-426* this permission was to be unfortunate.

After spending Christmas and New Year's Eve ashore, on home or local leave, the crew of the U-boat took it to sea again on 3 January for a second attempt in the North Atlantic. Five days later it had crossed the centre of the Bay and just about reached a point where the Bay joins the Atlantic ocean.

On a Bay patrol, looking for skulking U-boats was Sunderland U-Uncle of No 10 RAAF Squadron under the command of Coastal Command headquarters, operating out of Mountbatten. It was just before noon when the pilot of the flying boat, Flying Officer J. P. Roberts, had his attention drawn to a disturbance on the sea twelve miles on the starboard bow. Visibility at the time was fifteen to twenty miles and there was solid cloud at 4,300 feet and above.

The pilot altered course immediately and it was soon confirmed that a westbound U-boat was making twelve knots with its conning tower awash. It was this that had caught the eye. The lookouts in *U-426*, for this was the U-boat, had sighted the flying boat and a wrong decision was made to fight it out; at any time a U-boat was an unstable gun platform but with a rough sea it was more so.

The first shells were seen when the attacker was still five miles short of *U-426*, the flying boat dived under the ack-ack fire and replied at 1,200 yards with four fixed Brownings, and the pilot took successful evasive action round the curtain of flak. The first depth charge attack was abortive as the depth charge trolley failed to run out completely, but five or six dead or injured gunners were seen lying on the gun platform. The U-boat had meanwhile altered course ninety degrees to starboard, but once more made good a westerly course after the aircraft had passed over. At this stage Christian Reich did not carry out the instructions of the U-boat commanders' manual which read:

> If the aircraft has passed over without releasing its bombs submerge rapidly. Before the aircraft has turned to make a second attack, the U-boat will in most cases be already at depth.

The Sunderland made a steep turn and again attacked from the starboard quarter, releasing six Torpex depth charges spaced at sixty feet. The depth charges straddled the U-boat two to port and four to starboard. Huge plumes of water shot up, enveloping the U-boat in their spray. When they had subsided *U-426* had lost way completely and had a list to starboard. A little later it began to sink by the stern, and many of the crew were seen coming out of the conning tower. The aircraft then made another run firing all guns, but a minute and a half later the U-boat sank by the stern. Just after it sank there was an internal explosion in the U-boat, and immediately after the attack much oil and wreckage was seen. Thirty or forty survivors were left in the water. The fight was all over in seven minutes and for the Allies it demonstrated the value of a long continuous burst of fire at maximum range with the front guns.

The U-boat had transmitted a signal that it was being attacked from the air. Following the sinking of *U-426* and after another U-boat had been attacked and damaged Admiral Dönitz cancelled his previous permission to surface by day in the Bay.

CHAPTER TEN

An Inglorious End

'Where is the *Ark Royal?*' mocked Lord Haw-Haw from the German radio English language broadcast on the evening of 26 September 1939. The traitor William Joyce was to have the opportunity of asking this question many more times in the next two years and this question is still remembered as well as his opening announcement of 'Germany calling, Germany calling'.

The incident that prompted the question had taken place earlier in the day when the world's most famous aircraft carrier was attacked by a German bomber. The carrier's captain took avoiding action and a bomb fell 15 feet away. *Ark Royal* was shaken, anything portable was deposited on the deck, but no material damage was sustained.

Arriving back at base the German pilot reported that he had attacked an aircraft carrier in the North Sea and that a bomb had hit, or near-missed, the target. The German propaganda machine swung into action: the pilot was decorated and promoted, and against his will, a book was produced under his name entitled *How I sank the Ark Royal*.

In the next two years the carrier was involved in the South Atlantic incident when *Graf Spee* was scuttled, in the Norwegian campaign, the Oran incident and the chase for the *Bismarck*. Returning to the Mediterranean with Force H the carrier was employed ferrying Hurricane fighters to the hard-pressed island of Malta. While returning to Gibraltar on the afternoon of Thursday, 13 November 1941, *Ark Royal* was struck by a single torpedo fired from *U-81*. Early next morning the carrier heeled right over and sank. The U-boat had escaped.

The Type VIIC boat had been launched less than nine months earlier from the Bremer Vulkan yard at Vegesack. Oberleutnant Friedrich Guggenberger of the 1934 class was the first commander of *U-81*. By mid-July the boat had completed all the Baltic Sea training and was in Kiel awaiting its first war cruise. Leaving on the 17th, *U-81* sailed north, up through the Kattegat and Skagerrak, hugged the Norwegian coast and put into the beautiful base of Trondheim on 1 August. The U-boat carried out one short patrol from the 13th Flotilla base, which took it to the Kola area. The next patrol commenced on 27 August and took *U-81* to join with a pack of U-boats south of Greenland. Their target was a slow homeward-bound convoy of 64 merchant ships which were escorted by only one destroyer and three corvettes. By 9 September, with the convoy already round Cape Farewell, the pack struck – *U-81* opening the account with a moonlight sinking of the 5,591 ton *Empire Springbuck* by two torpedoes. The British steamer was 160 miles ahead of the convoy, probably because of the high explosive cargo it carried.

During the night *U-85*, *U-432* and *U-652* all made attacks and at dawn *U-81* sank its second victim, another British ship, the 3,252 ton *Sally Maersk*, with two torpedo hits. Three ships had been lined up in the sights and five torpedoes fired, but only one ship sank. Others in the pack, including *U-82*, *U-433*, *U-207*, *U-202*, *U-84*, *U-98* and *U-372*, registered successes and by the time fog came down on the afternoon of the 11th eighteen ships of convoy SC42 had been sunk. At the conclusion of the patrol *U-81* put in to Brest, on 19 September. Thus in less than three months *U-81* had been in three different U-boat bases in three different countries. The boat's crew spent only six weeks in France before being sent to another operational area, the Mediterranean.

Much to Admiral Dönitz's chagrin, Hitler had offered Mussolini twenty U-boats to help him keep open the lines of communication in the Mediterranean to assist the Italian forces fighting in North Africa. In October alone over sixty percent of the shipping despatched from Italy to Libya was sunk in transit. The Type VIIC boats were most suited to the Mediterranean conditions and *U-81* was one of the boats sent.

The boat left the Biscay base on 4 November and a week later it was ready to attempt the passage through the heavily defended Straits of Gibraltar at night. Each U-boat commander had his own ideas of entering the Mediterranean and most chose to pass on the fast flowing incoming tide. Guggenberger, now promoted to

Kapitänleutnant, was no exception. He chose to pass through on the night of the 11/12th on the surface and kept close to the European side, so close in fact that he was picked-up by a beam from the lighthouse that juts out from Tarifa at the most southerly point of Spain. The U-boat passed two fishing vessels and two destroyers but remained undetected, much to the relief of all. Once through the narrow strip of water *U-81*, together with *U-205*, was ordered to locate and attack heavy units of the Mediterranean Fleet, heading back to Gibraltar after supplying Malta with fighters. The force included the battleship *Malaya* and *Ark Royal*. Mastheads, identified as belonging to warships, were sighted and *U-81* moved into position. In mid-afternoon a four-torpedo salvo was fired and one hit the carrier.

Ark Royal was just thirty miles short of its destination, Gibraltar. At the time it had been landing-on aircraft in the afternoon sun. Those not actively involved in this operation were taking their tea and were all shaken when the carrier was hit amidships. The torpedo hit the starboard boiler room. Immediately all hands rushed to their action stations as the great ship heeled over to starboard. No broadcast orders were given as the power had temporarily failed. The list became more pronounced as there was no pumping machinery available to remove the water from the engine and boiler rooms on the starboard side. A call had gone out to Gibraltar for tugs and the destroyer *Legion* was skilfully brought alongside to take off most of the crew.

One seaman had been killed but all the remainder of the crew were saved. Early the next morning the carrier rolled over and sank. *Ark Royal* so often reportedly claimed sunk *had* been sent to the bottom by *U-81*. Initially the rest of the warships were more concerned with attending to the carrier, and the crew in *U-81* thought they had got away with it. Then came the asdic 'ping' as the destroyers found the U-boat, at 460 feet. More than 180 depth charges rained down in the next three hours but the U-boat escaped to join the 29th Flotilla.

The sinking of the carrier whose name had survived from the British flagship of the Spanish armada campaign started a grim period for the Mediterranean Fleet. Eleven days later *U-331* sank the battleship *Barham*, and her two sister ships *Queen Elizabeth* and

Valiant were badly damaged by charges from human torpedoes in Alexandria harbour on 18 December, the same day that the cruiser *Neptune* and the destroyer *Kandahar* were sunk in a minefield off Tripoli.

By this time the Americans had entered the war. In this same December month Hans Speidel joined the U-boat service. He had joined the Kriegsmarine in 1936 but two years later he transferred to the Naval Air Arm and later the Luftwaffe, He served in the western and eastern theatres of war attacking targets in France, England and Russia. After the necessary re-training Hans Speidel was appointed 1WO aboard *U-81* and took part in five Mediterranean operational patrols. The 2WO at this time was Oberleutnant Johann Otto Krieg, one of the 1937 class.

The next sinkings for *U-81* did not occur until mid-April when the U-boat was in the eastern Mediterranean. A 1,150 ton French steam trawler and the 6,000 ton British tanker *Caspia* were torpedoed and sunk ten miles south of Beirut on the 16th and later the same day three sailing vessels were set ablaze. Another was fired the next day, two on the 22nd and another four days later. Each victim was in the 80–100 ton category.

At the end of the following month Field Marshal Rommel started his attack on the Gazala Line and *U-81*, which was operating off Tobruk at the time, was ordered to search for the crew of a German aircraft who had taken to their dinghy after being shot down off the Libyan coast. Before the dinghy had been found another, more urgent, signal was transmitted to the U-boat. British aircraft from Nos 203 and 815 Squadrons had attacked and severely damaged *U-652* off Sollum and *U-81* was ordered to the position to assist. Steaming with both engines flat out *U-81* reached Kapitänleutnant Georg-Werner Fraatz and his stricken crew two hours later. As its engines were out of order a tow line was connected to the damaged boat with the intention of towing it to Piraeus. After some time the attempt had to be abandoned; the crew were transferred to *U-81* which now had 96 men aboard.

There then followed an action that must be unique in U-boat history: Georg-Werner Fraatz sank his own boat with a torpedo he fired from the stern tube of *U-81*. The U-boat that had sunk *Ark Royal* had now also sunk *U-652*! The date was 2 June and it had been sixteen months since *U-652* had been launched; it served in the Arctic, the Atlantic as well as the Mediterranean and sunk one destroyer, HMS *Heythrop*, three merchant ships and damaged two others.

On the next patrol of *U-81*, out of the Greek port of Piraeus, a commando party were taken on board with orders to destroy the rail links with Haifa, but this operation was cancelled at the last moment. The U-boat continued on patrol and on an early June morning, when west of Alexandria, *U-81* fired at an escort vessel and a tanker. The tanker was set ablaze. The last thing any U-boat in the Mediterranean wanted was heat from a fire, for the heat inside the boat was almost unbearable and the outside temperature in mid-summer was often in excess of ninety degrees Fahrenheit.

Hans Speidel left the boat to take his commanders' course and later commissioned *U-643*. Later the 2WO also left for the same course having served a full apprenticeship aboard the famous *U-81*.

Operation Torch, the invasion of North Africa, commenced on 8 November, and almost exactly a year after the sinking of *Ark Royal*, *U-81* found itself back in the same area. In the early hours of 10 November it attacked an escort vessel and a steamer. A red flash was seen from the escort and the British ship *Garlinge* was sunk. Other U-boats operating in the same area included *U-205*, *U-458*, *U-605*, *U-331*, *U-431*, *U-561*, *U-77*, *U-407*, *U-380*, *U-595*, *U-593*, *U-73*, *U-617* and Italian boats. The next success for *U-81* came in mid-afternoon of the 13th when two ships were attacked and the British motorship *Maron* of 6,487 tons was sunk. Four U-boats were lost between 12 and 17 November in the area: *U-660*, *U-605*, *U-595* and *U-331*.

This was also the last patrol in *U-81* for Friedrich Guggenberger who was already the holder of the Knight's Cross and was soon to be presented with the Oak Leaves.

The new commander of *U-81* was 'Hanno' Krieg who was delighted to take over command of the boat he knew and loved so well. He travelled down to Pola from Gotenhaven where he had been commander of the training boat *U-142* and took charge of the boat he had started with as 2WO on Christmas Eve.

On 5 February, not far from Tobruk, a mid-morning attack on a tanker was unsuccessful, two explosions were heard but the torpedoes were faulty. Four days later a small boat was sunk by

U-81

gunfire and the next evening a 6,671 ton Dutch ship *Saroena* was torpedoed. The next day four small boats, in convoy, were sunk by gunfire forty miles west of Tripoli. A month later, off Palestine, two more sailing vessels were sunk by gunfire on 20 March and a small Egyptian boat was torpedoed nine days later.

By now the Allies were mopping up the Axis forces in North Africa and U-boats were laying mines off Casablanca and in May they extended their minelaying to the coast of Greece, Sicily and Sardinia. On 12 May all organised Axis in Tunisia ended.

At sea again *U-81* had four successes to report on 26 June. First the 3,742 ton Greek steamer *Michalios* was torpedoed and sunk one mile west of Latakia and then three more sailing boats were sunk by gunfire.

On 10 July the Allies invaded Sicily, their first foothold in Europe. This meant plenty of work for the remaining U-boats. Since the Operation Torch campaign *U-224*, *U-443* and *U-83* had been sunk in the Mediterranean and others attempting to enter had been sunk before they could arrive. Within days of the Sicilian invasion the port of Syracuse had been seized and ships there were the next target for *U-81*. On the 21st a 12,000 ton supply ship was attacked but it was protected by a net defence and a torpedo was seen to hit the net. There was some consolation the next day when the 7,472 ton British steamer *Empire Moon* was damaged by a torpedo.

Early the next month *U-81* was the other side of the Mediterranean and in mid-morning of 6 August a target was attacked off Tobruk, four detonations were heard but no results were seen.

Bad news for the Germans came on 8 September when Italy surrendered and on 13 October declared war on its former ally. Although Tito's partisans had begun disarming Italian occupying troops a German offensive against the Yugoslavians meant that *U-81* was reasonably safe in Pola although the town's anti-aircraft guns were no longer manned.

On 18 November *U-81* was active in the area off the foot of Italy and the British steamer *Empire Dunstan* was torpedoed and sunk. This third *Empire* boat to be attacked was the last recorded success of Hanno Krieg who later in the year was awarded the Knight's Cross.

The Allied Strategic Air Force Command was bombing all enemy ports along the coast and on 9 January Pola was among the targets. The unprotected port was an easy target for a USAAF raid and *U-81* was destroyed and the nearby ex-Italian U-boat *Nautilo* was also hit. Fortunately for U-boat Command the commander was not aboard at the time.

This inglorious end to the successful U-boat was not immediately known to the Allies and it was not until an Enigma decrypt of the German naval key Porpoise that they could claim the destruction of the U-boat that with a single torpedo had sunk the Royal Navy's most famous carrier.

Friedrich Guggenberger, the former commander who had sunk *Ark Royal*, had later taken command of *U-513* and continued his success in the Atlantic until his boat was sunk following an aircraft attack off Santos in July 1943. He survived and became a prisoner-of-war.

CHAPTER ELEVEN

Repeat Performance

By the beginning of 1944 most of the U-boats had been equipped with the new 37mm fully automatic anti-aircraft gun. This weapon had a range of over 4,000 yards and a ceiling of some 12,000 feet.

The gun was fitted in a pivot socket mounted on the second gun platform abaft the conning tower. A depression rail was fitted to prevent the gunner hitting the superstructure of the boat when firing forward. The gun had an elevation of ninety degrees and could be depressed down to ten degrees. Normally the ring and bead sight was used but a telescopic sight could be substituted. The gun's crew consisted of five men; the trainer, who sat on the left, the gun layer who also fired the gun, on the right, the loader behind the gun, and two supply assistants. The gun was loaded by inserting clips of five rounds into the top of the breech block and fired by a pedal. The trainer and gun layer had received special training during an eight week gunnery and range-finding course at Swinemünde.

The men were protected by armoured shields 15-20mm thick, which folded back when the gun was secured in order to reduce water-resistance when the U-boat was diving.

The ammunition was orange tracer and self-destroying at 5,000 yards. Fifty clips of five rounds each were kept in ready use watertight lockers on deck. The cartridges had aluminium fuse heads which detonated on impact.

The breech block contained a chain which ran horizontally, like that on a bicycle. On the chain was a ratchet which pushed the cartridge into the breech. Prolonged submersion sometimes caused the chain to slacken, which was apt to cause a stoppage. All in all the anti-aircraft gun, in competent hands, was a formidable weapon with which to ward off aircraft attacks, and the gunners in *U-231* would shortly be given the opportunity to test their new weapon against an Azores-based aircraft.

By mid-January the Wellington crews were settling in at Lagens. They had arrived a month after the occupation of the Azores and now, two months later, had learned the various landmarks. Work was continuing on administration buildings and most of the officers and all the airmen were still quartered in tents in the various squadron dispersal sites. The planned nissen hut encampment on the north-east ridge was just being constructed, the main difficulty being that all stores, equipment and fuel had to come eighteen miles over an execrable road. Tunnelled into the slopes under the ridge were some small sheds which acted as squadron stores.

The Army and local population gave much assistance to the airmen, with Army bakers supplying new bread. One consolation was that local produce eggs, cheese, butter, pineapples and other fruit, all very short or unobtainable in the UK, were on the menu and the local wine somewhat made up for the lack of other alcohol.

The evening of Thursday 13 January was fine, with the moon two nights past full. At 1822 Wellington XIV L-Lucy HF168 of No 172 Squadron became airborne from Lagens airfield, flown by Pilot Officer W. N. Armstrong. The rear gunner was Flying Officer B. W. Heard who had joined the squadron three months earlier from No 1 PDC. The Wellington was on an anti-U-boat patrol, assisting the RN Escort Group 6.

After almost four hours' flying, at about 420 miles from base, a radar contact was made at ten miles, while the aircraft was flying at 1,500 feet.

Down below *U-231* was proceeding on the surface, charging its batteries, in conditions of low cloud and diffused moonlight.

The U-boat was a Type VIIC constructed at Kiel by the Germania Werft and launched at the beginning of October 1942. Kapitänleutnant Wolfgang Wenzel was in command; this was his first command and he had only joined the U-boat service earlier in the year after sailing in the secret raider *Atlantis*. Wolfgang Wenzel was navigator of the raider while it steamed 102,000 miles during its 622 days at sea under Captain Rogge. *Atlantis* sank 22 ships of nearly 145,700 tons. After twenty months at sea *Atlantis* was sunk by HMS *Devonshire* in November 1941. Along with many other survivors the navigator eventually returned to Germany and part of the journey was by way of rescuing U-boats. On 1 January 1942 the survivors all gathered in Berlin to be fêted by Hitler. Ten months later Wolfgang Wenzel had his own U-boat.

The singularly inglorious career of *U-231* commenced at Kiel on 13 April 1943, destination North Atlantic. In this first war cruise the boat was attacked by Fleet Air Arm aircraft on 12 May but managed to survive the fate that overtook 41 of its colleagues that were sunk in the month. Like the rest of the Atlantic U-boats, *U-231* was ordered to return and put in to La Pallice on the last day of the month. It ventured out again in July but was damaged by an RAF laid mine just outside the port and limped down to Bordeaux. It was from this more southerly base that its second proper war patrol began on 27 September; again North Atlantic convoys were the target. On 16 October *U-231* rescued five survivors of *U-964* which had been sunk following an attack by a Liberator. The U-boat returned to La Pallice on 22 November.

Many of the crew of the U-boat, now all qualified to wear the U-boat badge after 60 days at sea, were disappointed with the boat's lack of success; they felt their commander to be over-cautious, fearing air attacks. Only one torpedo was fired in the whole of *U-231*'s 121 days at sea, and that missed!

The third, and last, patrol commenced on Boxing Day from La Pallice, once more to the North Atlantic. On the night of 13 January *U-231* was with nine other U-boats in an area north-east of the Azores. The boats had been detailed to attack convoys on the Freetown-Gibraltar run.

All was tranquillity itself aboard *U-231* as its wake shone in the moonlight, attracting the attention of the crew of the Wellington above. Its diesels were propelling it at two knots while the batteries were recharging, but at the same time, the noise of the motors muffled the sound of the 1,735hp twin Hercules XVII engines of the aircraft.

Pilot Officer Armstrong flew into a position down moon of the radar contact. Having decided not to use his Leigh light in order not to draw attention to the Wellington, he was sure he had not been seen. He began to lose height and at 800 feet he was pleased to hear a shout through the intercom, 'U-boat ahead, sir.'

The U-boat was two-and-a-half miles away as the pilot dived straight in to attack from the port beam. The gunners were told to fire at any opportunity, not that they needed telling. There was no front power-operated turret on Leigh light Wellingtons and the twin Browning machine-guns were on a flexible mounting.

The white fan of *U-231*'s wake acted as a marker and the front gunner opened fire to deter the U-boat's gunners, but they were not expecting the attack. Bullets raked the decks and penetrated the forward torpedo compartment. Kapitänleutnant Wolfgang Wenzel rushed on to the bridge and all guns were made ready, but the concussion, or a hit, had jammed the training mechanism of the 37mm gun and put it out of action. As the aircraft turned, the rear gunner, who had also opened fire, saw the first depth charge explode close to *U-231* on the port side.

'There was a brilliant blue flash after the depth charges had come down,' said the pilot. 'I believe one of them may have hit the U-boat.' Actually the first fell 15 metres to port and the second two metres to starboard. Damage to the boat was considerable: the main switchboard caught fire, electrical equipment was damaged extensively, and water entered through the flanges of the stern torpedo tube.

The pilot then circled to port, intending to attack *U-231*'s port bow, but owing to cloud obscuring the moon, the U-boat was not sighted again until too late to attack. The U-boat was then seen to have turned through 180 degrees, lying stationary with its stern well down. The front gunner again opened fire, raking *U-231*, and the U-boat replied with machine-gun fire. A flame float was dropped immediately ahead of the U-boat's starboard bow.

The pilot reported of this second attack: 'The U-boat must have been too damaged to crash dive and our gunners opened fire immediately, raking all its visible parts; but it was ready for us and gave us everything it had; it was terrific and it was a miracle we weren't hit.'

Pilot Officer Armstrong again circled, but the moon once more became obscured, and the U-boat was not sighted although contact was maintained on radar. Another run-in was made and this time *U-231* was clearly seen by moonlight with the float flame slightly astern. It was still lying stopped with the after part submerged and bows well clear of the water. The remaining depth charges were now released in an attack from the starboard side. The pilot reported:

I came around for a third attack on the U-boat, which was clearly silhouetted in the moonlight. The hull aft of the conning tower was under water and the bows were well clear, proving that it was in no fit condition. And our front gunner fired with such success that the U-boat's crew only got off one round before they were silenced.

In fact the U-boat's gunners fired 80 rounds of 20mm. Hits were seen on the Wellington. Inside the U-boat the engineering officer reported that the boat was capable of diving and the captain gave the order to go down.

The Wellington pilot said the U-boat had disappeared after his last attack. Then, talking about the hit on the aircraft, he continued:

It hit the rear turret, smashing it and exploding in front of Flying Officer Heard. I didn't know about it at the time, and the first I learned of it was when I asked over the intercom what the rear gunner had seen of the attack.

Back came the answer: 'Sorry, sir, I'm afraid I must come out. I've been hit.'

'He showed the most amazing courage,' said the pilot, 'and managed to lever himself out of the turret with his arms.'

During the return trip to base Heard laughed and joked despite his pain. In addition to writing his report, Heard made diagrams of the attack in case he should not survive the trip. He was wounded with splinters in his left arm but his left leg was badly damaged. Back at base the emergency services had been alerted and as the Wellington touched down just before 0200 an ambulance was waiting to rush the gunner to hospital, where an amputation saved his life.

Back aboard the U-boat the gunners were hoping that their hit would stop the Wellington reaching base. In this they were disappointed, as they were again as their U-boat submerged. Partly because of water entering through the stern torpedo tube flange and partly because of damage to vents and pumps, *U-231* grew very stern heavy. The electric motors were turning only very slowly and could hardly hold the boat, which assumed an angle of 70 degrees. With difficulty *U-231* resurfaced for the last time; Kapitänleutnant Wolfgang Wenzel ordered the crew to abandon ship. 43 survivors were picked up the next day by the American auxiliary carrier *Block Island* and its attendant destroyers.

The last message U-boat headquarters had received from *U-231* had been transmitted on 12 January. Wolfgang Wenzel had been quite right to be apprehensive about air attacks!

Back in the Azores a signal came through confirming *U-231* as 'known sunk'. On 17 January the captain of L-Lucy, Pilot Officer W. N. Armstrong and air gunner Flying Officer B. W. Heard were given the immediate award of Distinguished Flying Crosses.

Observant readers will have noticed the No 172 Squadron Wellington HF168 was the very same one, flown by Squadron Leader R. G. Knott, the 179 Squadron detachment pilot, that sank *U-542* on 28 November. This Chester-built Leigh light Wellington certainly proved its worth, and in its way was reducing the number of U-boats available for the wolf packs.

CHAPTER TWELVE

Unseen Ends

At the beginning of December a large number of U-boats, chiefly from German bases, assembled off the North Channel and from the 5th to 15th they operated between 20 and 35 degrees West, as group *Coronel*, against ONS24, HX268 and ON215. German air reconnaissance, flown during this period by a maximum of two to three aircraft daily, failed to locate any of the expected convoys. On the 15th all available aircraft were sent west of the Bay of Biscay to reconnoitre for the previously mentioned blockade runners. In order to make use of this reconnaissance, group *Coronel 3*, which had gone far south in search of ONS25, was moved into the area west of Cape Ortegal. The remaining boats continued to search for convoys west of the British Isles, initially in three groups – *Sylt*, *Amrum* and *Föhr* – and from 22 December in six sub-groups of three boats each – *Rügen* 1 to 6. Instead of remaining in one position, these groups kept constantly on the move, changing their relative positions and opening out and closing in, so as to prevent the Allies from establishing the exact extent of the dispositions and leaving them only to perceive that the boats were scattered over a wide area. Actually this procedure brought some success, for as soon as the groups started to open out several convoys were encountered, two westbound on the 23rd and 30th, and an eastbound one on the 26th. In no case could the object of attacking with a minimum of three boats be achieved.

On 7 January these small groups were dissolved and the boats were allocated, singly, to attack areas west of the British Isles.

One of the boats, from a German base, was the Type VIIC *U-972*. It had only been launched at the end of February and Oberleutnant Klaus-Dietrich König quickly progressed his crew through the training exercises so that they were able to leave Kiel for their first patrol on 30 November, to the North Atlantic. The boat, with *U-960*, *U-392* and *U-744*, was ordered to proceed to the centre of the *Coronel* 1 group which then comprised *U-364*, *U-981*, *U-741*, *U-471*, *U-284* and *U-976* on 14 December. The next day *U-972* reported its position to U-boat headquarters and it was ordered from 1900 on that day to extend the patrol line. On 17 December *U-972* with five other boats comprised group *Sylt*. Five days later when *Sylt* and the two other groups were again divided *U-972*, *U-364* and *U-981* were to become one of the *Rügen* groups. Three times the patrol line was instructed to move to evade possible detection.

As mentioned above the groups were dissolved on 7 January and *U-972* was given an individual allocation. A week later the boat was ordered to a new position where it should have remained until 19 January. A new position was ordered two days later and on 23 January *U-972* should have set course for its new Biscay base.

Worried at receiving no signals from the boat, U-boat headquarters sent out the ominous signal 'Report your position' on 1 and 3 February. There was no reply. In fact the last message received from *U-972* had been on 15 December.

I have not been able to ascertain what happened to the U-boat. I have carefully examined all incidents involving U-boats in the six weeks from mid-December but none of them occurred at the right place at the right time. There is no question of sabotage as the boat had only been to Germany; it was too far from the coast to have entered a minefield. Whatever disaster overtook the boat must have happened very quickly for no distress signal was picked up by either side or by any other boat. The loss of *U-972* will probably remain a mystery.

The official conclusion of the Ministry of Defence is:

> The loss is unexplained. The groups in which *U-972* belonged were not involved in convoy attacks and there is no evidence that it was the victim of a stray T5.

Now to the story of a long-serving U-boat that until quite recently fell within the same mysterious category as *U-972*, but it is currently considered that *U-377* was the victim of a unique occurrence.

The Type VIIC boat was constructed at the Howaldts Werke at Kiel and launched on 12 August 1941. It was commissioned at the same port by Oberleutnant Otto Köhler on 2 October. The initial cruise from Heligoland on 17 February 1942 took the boat up to Norway where it joined the Arctic flotilla. The first two war cruises were two-week patrols from Narvik at the beginning of March and April.

The following month the Allies sailed 35 ships, the largest yet, in Russian convoy PQ16. *Admiral Scheer*, already at Narvik, was joined by the cruiser *Lützow* on 26 May. The previous day *U-377* had left the port in search of the convoy, and in fact was the first U-boat in touch and as such had the passive role of keeping the convoy in sight while other U-boats homed in. For its trouble the watch keeper was depth-charged and became one of five U-boats to be damaged while only one ship in the convoy was sunk. The U-boat put in to Trondheim on 29 May to be repaired and was there while the next convoy, PQ17, was scattered. Only 11 ships out of the original 35 arrived; many had been sunk by U-boats.

After its refit *U-377* left Trondheim on 18 July for a new destination. Both sides considered the northern island of Spitzbergen strategically important – the Allies for use as a flying boat base, to protect the Russian convoys, and the Germans for meteorological reasons. When *U-377* sailed it took five men of the 'weather corps' aboard to set up a secret weather reporting station on the island. While off the island the U-boat became completely ice-bound and supplies were taken ashore by sledge rather than by the more conventional rubber dinghies.

Arriving back to the beautiful scenery at Trondheim *U-377* was given a major refit, which took over a month, to repair the ice damage. Five days after the refit was completed on 3 September the U-boat put to sea to intercept PQ18, a Russian-bound convoy that had left Loch Ewe two days earlier. On the evening of the 16th *U-377* fired at a 7,000 ton steamer, a detonation was heard after 4 minutes 25 seconds, but the ship was not hit. Other U-boats were more successful, sinking three ships but three U-boats were also lost. The Luftwaffe also had some successes and only 27 of the original 40 ships reached Archangel.

When *U-377* returned on 23 September, its destination was Tromso, but it was only in port for two weeks before carrying out its sixth operational patrol, again in Arctic waters; this time there were no targets. The U-boat returned to Tromso on 23 October, but left again four days later, carrying out a patrol before returning south to Bergen, its fourth Norwegian base. Here, at Bergen, now with the 11th Flotilla *U-377* was given a two month major overhaul which lasted until the end of January 1943. The crew enjoyed the Christmas dinner inside the forward torpedo compartment of the U-boat.

Much to the relief of all in *U-377*, their eighth patrol was to the North Atlantic and nearly seven weeks later the boat put in to Brest. The first patrol out of the 7th Flotilla base took *U-377* to the area of the Azores. Here the U-boat found tranquillity while all around was chaos. U-boat command lost more boats in May than in any other month of the war and in consequence most of those at sea were recalled to base; *U-377* arrived on 7 June. The U-boat was taken in hand by the dockyard and was not operational again until 31 August.

There were on-going changes of personnel. The commander, Otto Köhler, had made good his commissioning promise of bringing the crew back safely and now moved on. His watch officer, Walter Pietschmann, had earlier left to take his commanding officers' course and now commanded *U-712*; later he took over *U-762* which was lost – he only survived his ex-crew members by 24 days. Ernst Gerke, known to his friends as 'Jumbo', was now the 1WO, and he took over while the boat was being refitted, giving the opportunity for the commander to go to Gotenhafen to witness a seaborne demonstration of a new weapon that was expected to revolutionise the U-boat war. The weapon was the T5, or gnat. This was a 21-inch electrically driven acoustic homing torpedo with a duration of 15 minutes having a homing radius of 300 yards. The torpedo was fired singly from a depth of not more than 70 feet. Four gnats were allocated to each boat going on operations, the aim was to sink the escorts so that the unprotected convoys could then be attacked conventionally.

The newly refitted, newly equipped *U-377*, under the command of Oberleutnant Gerhard Kluth was escorted out of Brest in the

U-377 returning to Brest for the last time in October 1943. (*Inset* the wounded commander Oberleutnant Gerhard Kluth)

early evening of 6 September. Soon afterwards a crew member fell overboard but was rescued and returned by the escort ship. Early the next morning a leak was discovered and *U-377* returned to port, only to be slightly damaged by the propeller of *U-256*. All was soon made right and two days later *U-377* finally set off to be one of 'twenty U-boats seeking two outward convoys.

When in position on the western side of mid-Atlantic, late on 20th, an R/T signal was received: 'Use radar impulses to find convoy.'

At the time starshells were visible. At 0341 on the 21st *U-377* unsuccessfully shot at a destroyer; the gnat detonation was heard three minutes and five seconds later. Soon after this another R/T message was received saying: 'Starshells are in the wrong place probably not the convoy.'

But by 0635 *U-377* had the convoy in sight and sent out an R/T signal giving its position. Soon fog came down and *U-377* was driven off by two Free French corvettes. When it resurfaced it sent reports to headquarters on attempts to get at the convoy.

In the early hours of the next day *U-377* had a fortunate escape as a destroyer came in to ram. Turning hard to escape, the U-boat's rudder jammed, but it was able to dive and then had the galling experience of hearing the convoy pass over. Surfacing an hour later, it sighted a steamer and another gnat was fired. There was a malfunction and it detonated after just 26 seconds. The U-boat was then depth-charged. In the early afternoon *U-377* surfaced. There was good visibility at the time and a four-engined aircraft was seen approaching; it was a Liberator from No 10 Squadron of the RCAF, based at Gander in Newfoundland. The U-boat opened fire immediately and at the same time sent the short signal 'Am being attacked by aircraft'. The attacker was driven off, but not before two members of the crew had been killed and the commander had been shot through both arms. He was losing blood and was taken below as the 1WO crash-dived. A further message was transmitted, requesting medical assistance.

Gunfire from *U-377* had been accurate, one of the aircraft's engines had been put out of action and the navigator wounded; he had a bullet in his leg and a slight scalp wound; however, the pilot was able to land safely.

Three days later, on the 25th, *U-377* was again attacked by

Crew aboard *U-377* awaiting arrival of the base commander

aircraft in the early hours. The attack was believed to be from a rocket-firing Swordfish from an escorting carrier. The hull was split and the conning tower bent, but fortunately the diving tanks were just missed. The boat turned hard to starboard, vibrating badly. It did not fully respond to controls. For the next two hours destroyer noises were heard above. After a long spell below, *U-377* cautiously surfaced just before midnight. All was clear, but with a wounded commander and a damaged boat the return journey was commenced. The boat arrived back in Brest on 10 October.

By 15 December Gerhard Kluth had recovered sufficiently to take his repaired boat to sea for what turned out to be its last patrol. The dispositions of the U-boats at this time are given at the beginning of the chapter. In mid-January an instruction issued from U-boat headquarters said: 'If a sighting is made at night boats are to press home their attacks regardless of enemy radar.' It appears that *U-377* was so employed when it sent a signal from west of the centre of the Bay of Biscay on 15 January.

The signal at 0404 said that it had fallen in with a hunter killer group which it had attacked with two T5's. An hour-and-a-half later, at 0539 the Admiralty picked up an emergency signal, the text of which was corrupt and the originator unidentifiable, to the effect that a boat had been struck by torpedo and was sinking. It was thought that the boat in question was *U-377* and had in the course of pressing home another attack on the group been hit by its own ₃nat. No other U-boat was operating in the vicinity of *U-377*.

U-boat headquarters did not receive its signal and this is probably why most reference books give the sinking of *U-377* as 'cause unknown'.

Bomber Command had to pay heavily for not hitting the Atlantic U-boat bases while the U-boat pens were being constructed. Once completed they were bomb proof and although thousands of tons of bombs rained down on them not one U-boat was lost in this way; the only ones to suffer were the French civilians, although they were usually warned of an impending raid.

Coastal Command were given the responsibility of sinking U-boats at sea, while Bomber Command were entrusted with the onerous duty of minelaying off the French bases. This took a lot of planning and diverted aircraft from what their Commander-in-Chief considered the main role of his force, bombing Germany. Many aircraft were lost on minelaying operations and it is problematical as to whether their rewards justified the risks involved.

One U-boat was sunk by an airborne mine on 20 January, this was *U-263*, a Type VIIC boat built at Vegesack by Bremen Vulkan and launched in March 1942. Kurt Nölke took it on its first patrol, from Kiel on 27 October for operations west of Gibraltar. Although it was unknown to the Germans, the Allies were at this time preparing to invade North Africa. Operation Torch saw American forces landing on 8 November and so *U-263* had been fortuitously sent to an area where action was almost guaranteed. Indeed, in mid-morning of 20 November *U-263*, in a position to the west of Morocco, intercepted a convoy that was reinforcing the landings. The commander fired a spread of torpedoes and four detonations were heard. The 7,000 ton Norwegian motorship *Prins Harald* and the British 5,000 ton steamer *Grangepark* were sunk and another was left burning. The convoy attack was the last for *U-263* for it was attacked by aircraft from Nos 233 and 405 Squadron and it limped in to La Pallice on 29 November. It was not until fourteen months later that *U-263* commenced its second patrol and this did not last long as it was sunk just one day out to sea by an RAF laid mine; all the crew were lost.

U-boat headquarters and the high ranking Korvettenkapitän Kurt Nölke of *U-263* had probably not realised that routine minelaying off the French Biscay coast had been continuous; indeed it intensified in the first quarter of 1944. A total of 422 aircraft laid 958 mines and 85 sorties were specifically carried out off La Pallice yet no aircraft were lost.

Earlier the laying of mines by aircraft in enemy coastal water could only be carried out successfully under very favourable conditions. It was necessary for the aircraft to make a certain pinpoint on some coastal land feature close to the release point, and then to lay the mines after making a timed run from this pinpoint. This demanded good visibility and an absence of low cloud. In addition, by virtue of the fact that landfall had to be made as close as possible to the release point, usually at low height, the aircraft invariably came within the range of enemy ground defences.

The clear presence shown by coast lines and the comparative ease of accurate interpretation of range and distance from prominent coastal features resulted in the development of a new technique. In January 1944 it was possible to release mines on H_2S independently from heights up to 15,000 feet, irrespective of low cloud and poor visibility. The release point for the mines was calculated for the most convenient heading of the aircraft, and the bearing and distance of this point from some prominent and convenient coastal landmark was measured before the flight. When the aircraft reached this position, as indicated on the tube on the required heading, the mines were released. The approach to the release point was chosen so as to provide for maximum assistance from H_2S while avoiding as far as possible heavily defended areas.

Minelaying, planting mines, was known in RAF parlance as Gardening. It was a thankless task, a great deal of effort for possibly little reward. The mine, really a type of delayed action bomb, flopped from the aircraft, floated down on its parachute, sank into the water, no splash, no flame and no flash. One pilot said, 'It's one of the most monotonous jobs in the world. You take your orders, fly for hours in the dark, reach the target area, drop the mines, then go back home. No thrills. No bangs. Just monotony.'

So three U-boats had been sunk in three weeks with no witnesses to their end and it was only through reading German signals that their losses were known to the British.

CHAPTER THIRTEEN

Bahr's Busy Boat

The operational life of *U-305* lasted less than a year but during this time it was an extremely active and busy boat and was involved in all its patrols.

The number, 305, gives the clue that this was a Lübeck-built boat as Flenderwerft secured the order to build thirty Type VIIC boats *U-301/U-330*. The first was launched on 21 March 1942 and the last in May 1944.

A week after the first launching a night air raid occurred that was to make 'a slight and temporary dent' to production in the port according to a German report. But in fact the raid on Lübeck, a Hanseatic city, was the turning point in the operational development of Bomber Command; it set out to demonstrate what area bombing could achieve.

The city, built on an arm of the Baltic, in the Schleswig-Holstein state, had its port surrounded by wooden houses and was thus selected as the target for a fire raid. For the first time the Avro Lancaster was used operationally in the 190 strong bombing force. The incendiary raid, according to Sir Anthony Eden, Britain's Foreign Secretary: 'Had a moral and dislocating effect out of all proportion to the direct military and economic importance to the city.' Dislocating effect or not, the construction of *U-305* was not too delayed as the yard had been turning out a U-boat every four weeks. *U-305* was duly launched on 25 July.

Kapitänleutnant Rudolf Bahr, who had served in *Prinz Eugen*, took command of the U-boat, which did not have to travel far for its Baltic trials. These were completed successfully but it was not until seven months after launching that *U-305* was ready to commence its first war patrol, from Kiel, on 27 February 1943.

Rarely could a U-boat have had such a baptism of fire on its first patrol, for it was assigned to the North Atlantic and was to play a significant part in the wolf pack operations in the convoy battles of the following month. A midshipman joined *U-305*, going aboard just 24 hours before it sailed; he was sea-sick for the first few days at sea and complained of being continually wet on his four-hour watch stints.

The boat, *U-305*, was the furthest north of a line of 26 U-boats waiting to attack homeward-bound Atlantic convoys, in particular SC122 and HX229. In all 40 U-boats were deployed. On St Patrick's Day the U-boat was fortunate to survive an attack by a Liberator which had approached to within a mile before it was sighted by Rudolf Bahr. The U-boat dived undamaged and managed to keep in touch with the convoy. In fact, at the end of 17 March only *U-305* was still in contact with SC122. Rudolf Bahr had steamed hard on the surface to overtake the convoy and then stopped and waited when some seven miles ahead. The boat was depth-charged four times by aircraft during the 17/18th and was forced to break off operations but the commander had executed the U-boat commanders' handbook instructions to perfection:

The object of every manoeuvre for improving the inclination is always the attack, which must be carried out as soon as possible, and an object of such importance must not be rendered more difficult to attain by lack of attention. It is therefore better, during the manoeuvre, to keep a little too far off than to be too close and thus expose oneself to the risk of being sighted and forced underwater, losing the advantage of attacking in time: delay the attack only in case of necessity . . .

. . . If it is not possible to improve the inclination by day; on acccount of air and naval patrol, put off the attack till night. Nevertheless, get ahead in good time by day. You should be abreast of the convoy at least by dusk. Do not put off till the evening the manoeuvres for improving the inclination. There is the danger of being forced by the manoeuvres of the rear escort to submerge or to withdraw, thus losing touch.

If the U-boat is forced to submerge for a time, owing to the enemy escort or for any other reason, it must not remain long under water. As soon as the situation permits, surface at once so as to forge ahead rapidly and reach the attacking position, and also so as to observe better and be able to transmit reports as to contact. It is possible to keep contact even if enemy naval and air escort are present. Conditions of attack are rendered more difficult by the presence of naval and air escort and it takes longer to prepare for attack. But with perseverance and tenacity on the part of the commander, it is certainly possible to keep contact. If he cannot succeed in preparing to attack by day, the U-boat must get to the point of firing by night.

When keeping contact, the greatest attention is necessary at the moment of transition between day and night, especially in the lower latitudes of the Atlantic where, with a very short twilight, one passes almost at once from day to night. The shadowing U-boat is, at nightfall, still almost as far from the enemy as during the day, and is suddenly obliged to close him at full speed. One must always remember that when it is dark the enemy may make a wide turn which, in addition to the zigzags observed up to then, will cause an appreciable alteration of the mean course, for the purpose of evading any U-boats which may be shadowing him. Besides which, especially at sunset (and possibly even by day if visibility deteriorates), the enemy will detach fast escort ships to reconnoitre the sea area astern of the convoy and force U-boats which may be shadowing to submerge, until the convoy is out of sight and has carried out unobserved its usual evening alteration of the mean course. These escort ships, detached for the purpose of driving off shadowing U-boats, always adopt misleading courses for their return.

Although twice being forced down by the air escorts during the day, when he was able to travel on the surface, Rudolf Bahr gave the engines in his new boat plenty of practice, making a steady sixteen knots and, as already recorded, was in an excellent position, seven miles ahead of the convoy at nightfall. The commander was also able to pick his attack position carefully allowing the approaching convoy to be silhouetted clearly in the bright moonlight. As the fifth and sixth columns of the convoy lines overlapped in the cross-wires of the periscope a two torpedo spread, fired at 2214, hit the *Port Auckland*

and *Zouave*. The latter, a 4,000 ton British steamer carrying a cargo of iron filings sank in five minutes. The 8,798 ton refrigeration ship took longer. Kapitänleutnant Rudolf Bahr had immediately dived after firing his torpedoes and on board his boat breaking up noises could clearly be heard as the boilers burst on the heavily laden *Zouave*. Two hours later, when the convoy had passed, the U-boat commander surfaced and the damaged *Port Auckland* was seen to be still afloat. Immediately another torpedo was fired and another valuable cargo of food and mail was lost to the Allies.

During the four day battles round the convoys 21 merchant ships were sunk and *U-305* on its first patrol had played its part to the full. After these heavy losses the United States made more escort vessels available for the Royal Navy to take over and sailed their auxiliary aircraft carriers to support convoy escorts on subsequent convoys. As shown in earlier chapters these two moves made certain that wolf packs would never again achieve the successes that *U-305* had assisted in on its first war patrol.

On 12 April *U-305* arrived triumphant at its French base. For most of the young crew it was their first time abroad and they were eager to get ashore; their dreams of French cooking, French wine and French girls were soon to be realised.

The U-boat joined the 1st Flotilla at Brest, the most northerly of the French bases, thus nearer to England than any other and within easy reach of the RAF and USAAF. For this reason barrage balloons were flown to protect the U-boat pens from low flying aircraft. The crew were billeted in the Naval college ashore while their U-boat was given an overhaul in the pens.

The boat and crew were given a clean bill of health and a month later Rudolf Bahr took *U-305* stern first into the shallow inner harbour then followed its escort vessel into the Bay of Brest before releasing it and continued on into the Bay of Biscay on its way to the North Atlantic. The U-boat was to join a pack seeking the eastbound 42 ship strong convoy HX239. Among the convoy escorts was the small carrier HMS *Archer*. On board the carrier three of its Swordfish aircraft had been converted to fire rocket projectiles, the first of the biplanes to do so.

On the night of 22/23 May H/F D/F reports suggested many U-boats, including *U-305*, were in touch with the convoy. Early next morning the convoy was 760 miles north of the Azores and at first light *Archer* flew off two Swordfish on anti-U-boat patrol. Later a Grumman Martlet single-engined aircraft was catapulted off. There were aircraft in the air at all times.

Reports of U-boats were coming in thick and fast. Lieutenant Tuke and his crew in a Swordfish reported an attack on a U-boat and so Sub-Lieutenant Nicholls with his crew and a Martlet were immediately scrambled. At 0845 the Martlet reported an attack on a second U-boat; this was also attacked by the Swordfish but the depth charges carried by this aircraft fell a little short although one was close to the U-boat, which had submerged so no results were observed. By 0900 the first RP Swordfish was ready for action and scrambled with Sub-Lieutenant Horrocks, Sub-Lieutenant Balkwill and Leading Airman Wish aboard. Soon afterwards a third U-boat was reported and attacked by Sub-Lieutenant Bowler in the Martlet. This U-boat was immediately again attacked by the rocket-firing Swordfish. This was the first rocket-projectile attack on a U-boat and was completely successful. The U-boat, *U-752*, caught fire aft and suffered severe damage to its steering gear during the rocket attack. Its commander had been killed by machine-gun fire from the Martlet. The Martlet made successful attacks on the second and third reported U-boats, both were astern of the convoy.

One of the U-boats attacked was *U-305* who reported being attacked by Fleet Air Arm aircraft, but it could equally well have been from a USN aircraft from *Bogue* whose task force were protecting a westbound convoy to the north. An Avenger dropped four depth charges on a U-boat and as *U-305* had its pressure hull damaged at the time this could well have been the U-boat attacked 26 miles from the convoy. The U-boat's gunners maaged to get off a few rounds before the depth charge plumes engulfed the boat.

Rudolph Bahr dived, made temporary repairs which held until *U-305* arrived back at Brest on 1 June and remained there for almost three months while the damage was made good.

During this time Kapitänleutnant Rudolf Bahr was ordered to Gotenhafen to attend a three-day practical course demonstrating the new acoustic torpedo. The commanding officers attending the course were taken to the middle of the Bay of Danzig in darkness and the new torpedo, known as the Gnat or T5 was demonstrated in action, using dummy warheads. This new 'escort killer' was meant to revolutionise U-boat warfare and for demonstration purposes the torpedoes were fitted with luminous dummy heads that could be seen in the dark. The torpedoes homed on to the loudest noise available; at sea this was the propellers of the escorts.

Like the others on the course Rudolf Bahr could hardly wait to get to sea again to try out this new weapon. It was 23 August, when the Bay of Biscay offensive was in full swing and many U-boats had been lost transiting the notorious Bay during the summer. The U-boat successfully made the difficult passage through the Bay and on into the North Atlantic.

Other U-boats headed out towards the northern shipping lanes in mid-September and *U-305* was one of twenty boats equipped with the new torpedoes. The German B.Dienst reported two westbound convoys, ONS18 and ON202, and the boats were ordered into a patrol line across their track. They were told to make the convoy escorts the primary targets, then the wolf packs could slaughter the helpless merchantmen.

On the evening of 20 September the two convoys were sailing quite close to each other and *U-305*, astern, did exactly as ordered and torpedoed the Canadian escort destroyer HMCS *St Croix* with an acoustic torpedo. However, the destroyer did not sink immediately so Rudolf Bahr gave it the *coup de grâce* an hour later. Following this *U-305* fired at HMS *Itchen*, but the frigate was not hit.

In all the U-boats sank six merchantmen and three escorts. Three U-boats were sunk in the five-day battle.

On 29 September *U-305* was one of 21 U-boats signalled into position to attack a westbound convoy, but the boat was unable to carry out its orders as it was attacked and damaged probably by an Icelandic-based Ventura of 128 US Navy squadron. It was on 2 October that *U-305* limped into Brest, damaged for the second time on two successive patrols.

Although the sinking of the six merchantmen and three escorts was a reasonable return the convoy figures reported to Admiral Dönitz were doubled as he was told twelve merchantmen and three destroyers had been sunk. He was delighted that his new acoustic torpedo attacks had been so successful. Hitler was also pleased; it was the only good strategic news being received in Germany at the time.

The U-boat spent two months in the pens at Brest while the damage to the boat was put right. The crew were transferred to their accommodation ashore before going on what would turn out to be their last leave.

On 8 December *U-305* left its Biscay base for the last time, destination again the North Atlantic. At the time the U-boat left five surface ships were attempting to beat the Allied blockade and bring in much needed cargoes from the Far East to Biscay ports. Unwittingly *U-305* was to help cause the destruction of probably the most important of them. In mid-November U-boats had been instructed not to attack independent ships sailing in the South Atlantic; this had been decrypted by Enigma. Further decrypts revealed more information as the ships approached German occupied territory. A US carrier group, led by USS *Card* was searching for the blockade runners and *U-305* was one of a pack of thirteen U-boats instructed to act against this task force.

On the night of 23/24 December the U-boat was the first to sight the Americans but was picked up on radar by escort destroyer USS *Schenck* and forced to submerge. While the task force and U-boats took on each other the blockade runner *Osorno* was fast approaching France and it reached the mouth of the Gironde. The ship was beached after hitting a submerged wreck but its valuable cargo of rubber was subsequently unloaded.

The Admiralty had received no information about *Alsterufer*, probably the most important of the blockade runners, later it transpired it had been delayed by adverse weather in the Atlantic. At 2,700 tons *Alsterufer* was the smallest but fastest and most heavily armed of the blockade runners. The crew had confidently expected to be back in Europe for Christmas and most of them had purchased their gifts while out East. It was at noon on Christmas Day that the ship was sighted well out to sea by *U-305*. Rudolf Bahr quickly had a message sent off in the top secret officers' code. Decrypting of such a top priority message took precedence over everything and an hour after transmission the British officials at Bletchley Park were able to inform the Admiralty that *U-305* had signalled U-boat control that it had sighted *Osorno*. The following day a signal from U-boat headquarters revealed that the ship *U-305* had seen was *Alsterufer*, not *Osorno*, and this was the news that the Admiralty was waiting for. A task force was already at sea, Coastal Command had its aircraft fuelled up ready to take off and depth charges were loaded on some aircraft and bombs on others. A heavy aircraft attack with rockets, bombs and depth charges set *Alsterufer* alight on the 28th and the ship was abandoned. Of the blockade runners only *Osorno* arrived back, the others being sunk or scuttled.

Still on patrol, *U-305* was one of a group of U-boats well out in the Atlantic awaiting convoys but the Admiralty knew where they were and on 7 January a support group was sent to attack them. Once again it was *U-305* that scored the first success, sinking the frigate HMS *Tweed*. Actually the frigate was just returning from hunting blockade runners. The action took place in the late afternoon and the frigate sank in four minutes. HMS *Vasketh* was quickly on the scene and carried out two depth charge attacks but *U-305* remained undamaged.

That same day, 7 January, may well be regarded as the day that the *Rudelsystem* was abandoned as the U-boat war diary entry for the day says:

> One boat will now have to attack the whole escort and after discovery endure the enemy counter measures alone . . . a successful mass U-boat campaign with existing types and those planned for the future is only possible if the boats are directed to the convoy by continual air reconnaissance.

On the evening of the 8th *U-305* was right at the end of a patrol line when it sighted convoy OS64/KMS38. The convoy was shielded by Escort Group B4, which included HMS *Abelia*. The corvette had joined the convoy at daylight on 5 January. At 0427 four days later she picked up a contact astern of the starboard wing column at a range of 2,800 yards. This was *U-305*. The corvette captain immediately reduced speed to 7 knots and at 1,700 yards the contact was confirmed as a U-boat. At the time the ship was not streaming its foxer gear; her captain thought that with the wind force 5/6 and heavy seas commencing to break, with a falling glass, a full gale was in the offing and so did not stream his noise-making gear. It had been his original intention to stream paravanes at dawn.

Closing the contact *Abelia* increased to full speed. When she was just under a thousand yards distant, at 0435, a ten pattern charge was dropped and all the depth charges fired. At about the time of entry of the third charge from the rails into the water, a heavy explosion occurred fine on the starboard quarter, blowing off the rudder, partially flooding the tiller flat.

Rudolf Bahr had struck again, making the escort his primary target, his gnat had proved its worth just at a time when the U-boat itself was under attack.

The now damaged *Abelia* continued to act as directing ship while others of the escort searched for *U-305*. They were unsuccessful. The rest of the U-boat group were ordered to attack but as they had been dispersed at wide intervals none succeeded in closing.

The corvette did not know what hit her. As she was taken in tow by the tug *Storm King* and course set for Milford Haven, her captain produced a report of the incident. He thought there was a faint possibility that one of his own depth charges, set too shallow, might have caused the explosion; he did not exclude a torpedo, but said, 'If a gnat is taken into consideration I am confident that at no time during the attack was the U-boat end on to the ship.'

Two days later another of the escorts, the corvette HMS *Lunenburg*, was hit by *U-953*.

In mid-January, using the new single boat strategy, *U-305* was one of two dozen U-boats deployed in an arc from the Faroes to Brittany about 250 miles out from the British Isles. They were disposed in twenty to forty mile wide attacking areas, moving by day at periscope depth and surfacing at night only to recharge their batteries.

It was on 13 January that *U-305* received its orders for the new dispositions and two days later it contacted U-boat headquarters, possibly to inform them it was in position 420 miles west-south-west of Cape Clear.

Passing through this same area two days later, the 17th, was Escort Group B1, returning home after their search for the blockade runners, that had now all been accounted for.

The Group was disposed in line abreast three miles apart spread from left to right *Glenarm, Wanderer, Woodpecker* with the Senior Officer aboard, and *Watchman*.

The frigate *Glenarm* had only been launched from the Scottish yard of H. Robb of Leith ten months previously and it will be remembered that less than a month earlier she had rescued the crew of HMS *Hurricane* on Christmas Day and that among those rescued was Signalman John Kennedy who says:

> Much to the surprise of everybody, I was not particularly keen on going back to barracks and wanted to stay at sea, even forgoing survivor's leave. As a result I learned that one of the signalmen on board *Glenarm* had eye trouble and was to be replaced when the frigate returned to the UK. I volunteered to replace this crew member and after, I believe, some signals with the Admiralty, this replacement was authorised.

The next ship in the line was HMS *Wanderer*, an old V and W Class destroyer launched in 1919, which had the pendant number D74 until 1940. Along with others of her Class *Wanderer* was converted to a long-range escort, when she became I74. In the summer of 1941 she sank *U-147* and *U-401*, with the help of other vessels. In January 1943 *Wanderer* entered Devonport dockyard where the forward boiler was removed and the boiler room converted to a fuel tank to provide additional endurance which enabled her to cross the Atlantic without refuelling. With the fore-funnel removed and 'A' gun replaced by the hedgehog and with Oerlikon gun armament augmented the old vessel was almost on a par with newly constructed escorts when she returned to sea in May 1943.

On board *Wanderer* was Coder Robert Mendoza, who recalls:

> As a coder I sat alongside the telegraphist, decoding as the signals were arriving – which were constant. Many signals were irrelevant to us, I decoded the call signs to see if the signal was either direct to *Wanderer* or to a group of ships in the specific area in which we were or which we were intended to pass through. During action stations I was required to be up on the bridge with the Captain so that he could see what was happening at the very moment I was decyphering or decrypting.

Another rating aboard *Wanderer* was acting Able Seaman H. W.

Houston. It was his sharp eyes that saw *U-305* at 1355. At the time visibility was only five miles in the south-south-west force 5–7 wind. The Group were steaming at twelve knots.

A first sighting report was signalled, and *Glenarm* and *Wanderer* as the two nearest ships were sent to attack while *Woodpecker* and *Watchman* protected them. *Wanderer* increased speed to 18 knots and picked up a contact at 1,200 yards. Depth charges had been set to 100 feet and five were dropped at 1400, but the destroyer was going too fast and the target turned to port at the end of the attack and the pattern probably missed ahead.

The hedgehog ahead-throwing missiles were readied and nine minutes later a pattern was fired. Ten minutes later an underwater explosion was heard, although obviously after such a long time gap this could not have been one of the missiles hitting *U-305*.

At 1500 it was *Wanderer* who again attacked, although the echo had been lost at 700 yards. A ten depth charge pattern was dropped with the settings of 150 and 300 feet and at the time it was thought that the charges had not been set deep enough.

The first attack from *Glenarm* came at 1546 when the hedgehog was fired. The ship's officers were certain that the pattern was fired much too early, at 330 yards, and probably missed ahead. Five minutes later *Wanderer* attacked again in the same spot, dropping ten depth charges set at 250 and 385 feet. It was thought they may have missed to starboard as the target drew to starboard at the end of the attack.

Up until this time only the captain of *Wanderer* was sure that he was attacking a U-boat; the others were not convinced. Looking for tell tale signs of destruction *Woodpecker* sighted a piece of flotsam and recovered a spar, but when it was found to be covered with barnacles it was returned from whence it came.

Glenarm made her first depth charge attack, directed by *Wanderer*, at 1625. Ten charges were dropped, set at 350 and 550 feet but it was considered that they were not correctly dropped for depth and range.

It was nearly three hours before the next attack came. Down below the crew of *U-305* had been keeping silent routine as the propellers of their four hunters were heard thrashing the water. At 1916 in the heaviest attack so far, *Wanderer* dropped sixteen depth charges set for 350 and 500 feet. They were probably fired late, for the U-boat turned to port.

A hedgehog attack was next mounted from the destroyer at 1950. No hits were achieved and *U-305* turned sharply to port – its crew had just over an hour to live.

For some unexplained reason the motors of *U-305* increased speed at 2045, revealing its exact position to the waiting *Wanderer*. The forward thrower had been reloaded and a hedgehog attack eleven minutes later sealed the fate of *U-305*.

An underwater explosion occurred 15 seconds after launching, this indicated that the target was at 175 feet. Still no evidence of destruction came to the surface. Although the U-boat had increased speed the underwater speed could only be described as slow, so the report stated that *Wanderer*, herself steaming at 10 knots, made a perfect attack on a slow moving target.

The Group still were not certain of their success. *Wanderer* searched the area to westward, the area to the north and east being covered by the remaining ships. At 0117 the hunt was abandoned due to deteriorating weather conditions.

One person who was extremely pleased when the stand down was given was Robert Mendoza:

> I recall the action and sinking of *U-305* as it was one of the longest periods of 'no-sleep' for me. I had just come off watch when we made first contact with the U-boat, and was called back to action stations. Prior to that watch, when I should have been off duty, we had had two false alarm action stations so I had no rest for some fourteen hours prior to making the contact, followed by twelve hours in contact with the U-boat, making a total of over 26 hours on duty without sleep – for me this was a record.

In a space of under two months John Kennedy, now on *Glenarm*, had joined his first ship, had the trauma of her being sunk and now the elation of his new ship sinking a U-boat. He continues:

> During a period of intensive action, with many signals to and fro, our RN Commander called out, 'Signalman'. I responded and he said:

'Ah, Kennedy, how old are you?'

'Seventeen, Sir,' I replied, to which the Commander said:

'You're a good lad, Kennedy, but send for the Yeoman of Signals.'

A come-down for me, but of course, with hindsight, I realise the wisdom of the Commander's action. I suppose he thought, too much responsibility for one so young. I spent my 18th birthday on a Russian convoy – by this time the name of *Glenarm* had been changed to HMS *Strule*.

The hunting group reached Londonderry and submitted a report of the action. It was suggested that after the final hedgehog attack, when the underwater explosion was heard, it might have been a good idea to send down a couple of depth charges set to 175 feet to see whether this would have brought up any evidence of destruction.

At this time the assessment was ' probably sunk'. Confirmation was not long in coming. A call for *U-305* to report its position went unheeded and the British were to learn as soon as the Germans that another potential ace had been lost with his boat.

HMS *GLENARM*

Rudolf Bahr had achieved remarkable results with his boat. On his first patrol, at the end of the line, he had been the only U-boat commander to keep in contact with the convoy; he then sank two merchantmen and returned to base with little fuel remaining through continual diving. On his second patrol it escaped Fleet Air Arm aircraft attacks. On the third patrol it sank one escort and fired at another and was damaged by an aircraft attack returning to base.

On its fourth patrol one of *U-305*'s sharp-eyed look-outs first saw one of the blockade runners. It sank another escort, escaped detection and later hit another escort with a gnat. The boat always found the action.

The U-boat could consider itself unlucky to be in an area where a Group were returning to harbour. The ships were strung out covering a nine mile width, and with visibility five miles it meant that *U-305* had to be within a 19 mile swathe to be sighted. When sighted it was only *Wanderer* initially that was certain there was a U-boat. Rudolf Bahr made no signal, there was no point, no U-boat was close at hand and a signal could have been D/F'd giving away his position for certain.

After forty days at sea, and still 500 miles from base without being refuelled *U-305* would soon be expecting its own recall. The possibility was that all its gnats had been expended with the attacks on HMS *Tweed* and *Abelia*; there was therefore nothing the U-boat could sensibly do once it had been located.

Probably the hydroplanes of *U-305* had picked up the sound of the four warships' propellers long before it was sighted and that once the sound of four ships moving at twelve knots had been heard the worst must have been feared and Rudolf Bahr came up to confirm that it was warships that were approaching. Really he had no reasonable chance of escaping, except to keep quiet hoping he would not be located.

After *U-305* had successfully escaped the first eight attacks the increase of speed detected at 2045 must remain a mystery. The U-boat commanders' instructions specifically said, 'Avoid a high speed since the loud noises of the propellers in the water can be picked up.' If there had been a blowing of tanks, indicating the U-boat was surfacing hoping to escape in the night it would have made sense, but the increase of speed effectively sealed the fate of Rudolf Bahr and his crew who had fought independently and with the pack with great resolution.

Other U-boats were soon to suffer *U-305*'s fate to the west of Ireland.

CHAPTER FOURTEEN

West of Ireland

Two days after *U-305* was sunk *U-641* followed. The Type VIIC boat was launched from the slip of the Blohm and Voss yard at Hamburg on 6 August 1942; Kapitänleutnant Horst Rendtel was its commander.

The boat, launched a month after *U-305*, also set out on four war patrols, but unlike *U-305* achieved very little although it was often in areas where others with it were registering successes.

On its first war cruise, out of Kiel, the opportunity of success could not have been better. Passing up through the Danish sea, after leaving Kiel on 20 February, the boat was assigned to the North Atlantic, where some of the fiercest convoy battles were soon to be fought, with the balance of success tilted the way of the U-boats.

In mid-March, with three eastbound convoys at sea, one of them was sighted and a large concentration of U-boats was ordered to a position in the air gap, an area where no air cover could be provided for the convoys. Although brief contact was made with convoy SC122, *U-641* did not make any attacks. The U-boat signalled U-boat headquarters that it had been the target of an aerial attack, which was impossible. What *U-641* thought were depth charges being dropped were in fact torpedo detonations of another U-boat's successful attack on the convoy.

On 10 April *U-641*, still with a full complement of torpedoes, entered St Nazaire and joined the 7th Flotilla at the French base. It had missed out on what was to be the U-boats' best month in the North Atlantic. The boat was in the pens for just over four weeks before setting out again on 9 May for the Atlantic, to an area southwest of the Azores. Once more *U-641* missed out, but this time it was a good miss as more U-boats were sunk in May than at any other month. The boat was at sea for two months before returning on 16 July, with no results to report.

The third patrol was supposed to be off the west coast of Ireland but it extended out to the Atlantic. The patrol commenced on 4 September and six days later *U-641* attacked a destroyer escorting convoy ON202, but no hit was registered. On 29 September *U-641* was one of 21 U-boats signalled to move to a position where a convoy was expected in two days, unfortunately for the U-boats their signals were being read and the convoy was so routed as to avoid them.

A signal addressed to sixteen U-boats, including *U-641*, on 6 October ordered them to a new position to intercept convoy SC143. What U-boat headquarters did not know was that two of the U-boats to whom the signal was addressed had already been sunk.

The convoy was intercepted and both sides suffered losses with U-boats and destroyer escorts being lost. In the early hours of 8 October *U-641* was close to the convoy and reported seeing searchlights. Later it reported being sighted by an aircraft, possibly a Swordfish from the MAC ship *Rapana*. On the afternoon of the 9th all boats that could be ahead of the convoy by dawn were ordered to do so and the rest were withdrawn to the westward. It was then that the only ship lost in the convoy was torpedoed, by *U-645*. At the end of the patrol *U-641* again returned to St Nazaire, for the last time, with no sinkings to report. It must have been depressing for the crewmen, who had all now qualified for the U-boat badge having spent over sixty days at sea, to chat with their colleagues in their quarters at La Baule and have no successes to talk about.

For the majority of the crew, and certainly all of them that were to embark for the fourth patrol, it was their last leave. Kapitänleutnant Horst Rendtel conned *U-641* from its base on 11 December, knowing he would not be back for Christmas, but was entirely unaware he would not be returning at all. His patrol area was the North Atlantic.

Just before Christmas *U-641* was in one of six sub-groups of three U-boats each. Instead of remaining in one position, these groups kept constantly on the move, changing their relative positions and opening out and closing in, so as to prevent the Allies from establishing the exact extent of the dispositions. This procedure brought some success as an eastbound convoy was intercepted on the 26th and two westbound, on 23 and 30 December. However, in no case could the U-boats achieve their object of attacking with a minimum of three boats, thus the sole remaining argument in favour of dispersal in small groups was disproved.

The fact that the virtual discontinuance of pack attacks would further diminish prospects of success had to be accepted and henceforth single U-boats had to come singlehanded with the entire convoy escort and bear the brunt of its counter attack.

This was the situation then when *U-641* was the first U-boat to gain touch with convoy OS65/KMS39 that the U-boats had been ordered to find. The convoy was located on 19 January off Ireland, 360 miles west of Cape Clear.

The finding of the convoy was probably *U-641*'s biggest achievement and in fact it was carrying out orders and had submerged ahead of the convoy. It was here, in the evening, that the U-boat was located despite a heavy sea running, in a westerly gale.

Included in the convoy's escort, B3, was HMS *Violet*. John Cannon had recently joined the Flower Class corvette when it put in at Sheerness dockyard when oerlikons were fitted. After this, in November 1943, it sailed north to the Inner Hebrides. Here it had to pass the close scrutiny of Commodore Gilbert Stephenson, known as the 'Terror of Tobermory' before it was allowed to proceed on operations again.

John has reason to remember these days. After his initial training at *Ganges* he came down to HMS *Wildfire* at Sheerness and from this shore station he joined *Violet*. While on the trials the magazine lid of an oerlikon fell on his hand as the ship executed a quick turn.

After the trials *Violet* spent a few hours in Londonderry before picking up the convoy. Seaman John Cannon says it was a three ring escort, with *Violet* being in the outer ring. It was in this position that *Violet* located *U-641*, ten miles ahead of the convoy in the early evening.

The asdic operator reported the echo and later confirmed it as a U-boat. The corvette captain reduced speed to 5 knots. Slow speed was maintained as *U-641* was heard turning away, asdic conditions were good.

The captain decided on a hedgehog attack and increased speed to 8 knots before firing off the first pattern. This was released 220 yards ahead and after an interval of sixteen seconds two, almost simultaneous, explosions were heard. A third followed two seconds later, indicating that three of the 24 projectiles had hit. Contact was temporarily lost after the explosions but was later regained despite the considerable water disturbance in the vicinity. At 1935 an oil patch was observed and three minutes later *Violet* carried out a second hedgehog attack. After passing over the contact a violent muffled explosion was heard by all on deck and in the engine room. This explosion was confirmed to have come from astern, almost certainly it was the last desperate action of *U-641*'s commander, firing a gnat at his attacker. By the time the end of range gnat explosion occurred *U-641* had probably been destroyed, as breaking up noises were reported by the engine room staff.

Up top there was a strong smell of fuel oil and this was considered by the engineering officer to be diesel. This opinion was backed up by an ERA. The oil patch spread over an area covering one by one-and-a-half cables. Efforts were made to obtain a sample by trailing a canvas sack through the oil, but it was not possible due to the heavy sea. *Violet* rejoined the convoy and *U-641* joined the company of many other U-boats that had not registered any successes against the enemy.

The Atlantic U-boats moved nearer to the coast of Ireland. They disposed singly moving by day at periscope depth, or at a suitable depth for hydrophone listening, so as to be able to receive W/T messages on longwave.

Among the searching U-boats was the Type VIIC boat *U-271* under the command of reserve officer Kapitänleutnant Curt Barleben, a graduate of the Kriegsmarine class of 1935. The boat had been built at the Bremer Vulkan yard at Vegesack and launched toward the end of July 1942. The convoy successes of March and the U-boat losses of May had occurred before *U-271* commenced its first, uneventful, patrol from Kiel on 29 May. On completion of the North Atlantic patrol *U-271* put in to Lorient but later made the short journey up the Brittany coast to Brest. At the French naval dockyard *U-271* was one of the few boats that were converted to flakboats. Three such boats operated with packs in the Bay and off the Iberian coast but on 2 October *U-271* was sent out to an area north of the Azores. Just a month later *U-271* returned to Brest with no successes to report. The crew spent a long time ashore at the

French base, including leave over Christmas and the New Year, while the extra flak armament was removed and it was not until 12 January that *U-271* put to sea on its third patrol and linked up with other U-boats.

Along with others in the group *U-271* had the following order:

> If by day the enemy is sighted through the periscope or located by hydrophone, boats are either to attack at once, or surface to gain bearing and make an enemy report. Contrary to previous practice, however, they are to break off the operation and submerge on the appearance of strong enemy air forces, or if weather conditions are such as to hinder the firing of the anti-aircraft armament or expose the boat to danger of surprise attack through low cloud. If there is a possibility of catching up with the target that night, boats are to pursue at high speed.
>
> If a sighting is made at night, boats are to press home their attack regardless of enemy radar or air opposition.
>
> On receipt of an enemy report by day or night, all boats favourably situated are to make every effort to gain contact with the enemy, operating in the manner laid down for the single boat.

Two days after *U-271* sailed, on 14 January, the searching boats after several changes of position were brought closer in to the North Channel, where the Allied air and sea defences proved tolerable and the boats managed to close in slowly as far as 15 degrees west. From their few sightings and radio intelligence reports, it was apparent to the Germans that the Allied forces were evenly distributed over the whole area and not concentrated at specific points and that convoys were circumventing the U-boat disposition to the north and south. For this reason the boats on the northern and southern wings of the disposition were wheeled, respectively, to the south-east and north-east, so as to form a semicircle round the North Channel covering the presumed outward and return routes of the convoys. Yet, despite this precaution contacts remained few, and many single ships and convoys passed the U-boats' disposition unnoticed.

The movement of the U-boats off Ireland was reported to the Admiralty and Coastal Command's 15 Group was reinforced by Leigh light Wellingtons, and Liberators of 19 Group, moving to

Northern Ireland airfields. By this time two groups of eleven and eight U-boats were 270 miles off Malin Head awaiting convoys and just after midday on the 25th *U-271* sighted a destroyer and fired a gnat. An end of run detonation was heard after eleven minutes. On the 26th convoy KMS39 was sighted west of the North Channel, and eight of the southern boats of the group, including *U-271*, were formed into a patrol line at the position through which the convoy was expected to pass at sunset on the next day. As there also could have been an outward convoy to the westward of the British Isles the remainder of the group of U-boats were hurriedly assembled in a smaller area north-west of the North Channel.

The Luftwaffe had reinforced the Fliegerführer Atlantik bringing his force up to eleven Ju290s, two BV222s and four long-range Ju88s. U-boat headquarters requested the Luftwaffe to report the convoy's position at regular intervals, so that they could detect any deviation in good time, but the radio transmitter of the Ju290 that flew the night reconnaissance on the 26/27th broke down, and it was not until the afternoon of the 27th that the early morning positions were received by the U-boat command and these indicated a pronounced westerly course. Had the position been transmitted when sighted the patrol line could have been moved ahead of the convoy under cover of darkness. When a later report from a relief aircraft gave the convoy's position as even further west, those boats carrying 3.7cm anti-aircraft gun protection were ordered to surface and close the convoy at high speed, so that they should be favourably situated to receive the aircraft's homing signals at dusk.

The British listening services monitoring the Luftwaffe reporting the position of convoys ON221 and OS66/KMS40 on the 27th passed on the information they gained and soon a squadron of Beaufighters from 19 Group moved to Northern Ireland to discourage the Luftwaffe aircraft.

The BV222 that the U-boats were instructed to listen for at dusk had some bad luck. It had taken off in the morning for the evening reconnaissance but had to return at midday because of engine trouble and so the wireless operators on the U-boats twiddled their knobs in vain at dusk straining their ears to pick up homing signals that were never sent. Just after midnight the next Luftwaffe aircraft made contact with the convoys but, owing to a technical defect, was unable to send homing signals and the U-boats searched throughout the night without gaining touch in the prevailing bad weather and visibility. The bad weather, coupled with fog at their bases, kept the Coastal Command aircraft on the ground that night.

The 28th turned out to be a bad day for the U-boats that had been ordered to surface and chase convoy ON221. It was a windy day with a heavy sea running in the North Channel and it was probably due to these factors that the lookouts on *U-271* did not see an aircraft approaching. The strong wind, combined with spume blowing into their eyes left a vital sector in which they could not search and this allowed Liberator E-Easy of 103 Squadron US Navy to approach their boat unseen 210 miles west of Blacksod Bay, to the west of Limerick. The bombing support squadron Liberator, under the control of Coastal Command, was on an anti-U-boat patrol when it saw the U-boat in the early afternoon. The U-boat was sighted at eight miles on the starboard beam of the Liberator. The boat was estimated to be making ten knots, at the time the wind was blowing at 40 knots. The American pilot immediately turned his Liberator ninety degrees to starboard and approached out of the sun. The gunners in the U-boat could only have sighted the Liberator at the last possible moment as only a few bursts of flak were encountered as the attack commenced. No hits were made on the aircraft whose gunners replied vigorously from the front and beam guns.

The Liberator tracked over the U-boat's port beam forward of the conning tower and released six depth charges from fifty feet, spaced at fifty feet. Explosions straddled *U-271* abaft the conning tower, four to port and two to starboard. The stern lifted, then settled, and all forward movement was lost. As *U-271* settled lower the surrounding water was filled with air bubbles. After circling twice the American crew lost *U-271* in the very high seas that were running at the time. Passing over the estimated position the aircrew saw a light green patch of swirling water filled with air bubbles. Probably due to the high waves no wreckage or oil was seen. The Liberator continued to patrol the area for another forty minutes before flying off to report the attack to the SNO of the convoy some 38 miles away. The Liberator pilot was ordered to patrol the area until a relief Liberator and a corvette arrived. When relieved E-Easy set course back to Dunkeswell.

The U-boat and its crew were all lost. All that it had achieved was an abortive gnat attack on a destroyer three days before it was sunk. The last message U-boat control received from *U-271* was on 28 January, probably reporting the aircraft attack just before it was sunk.

The next U-boat to be lost was also pursuing the outward-bound convoy on the surface when it was spotted by the front gunner of a Sunderland.

The Type VIIC U-boat was *U-571*. It had been an active boat since its launch from the Blohm and Voss yard in Hamburg at the beginning of April 1941. It was commanded by Helmut Möhlmann, who was later to be awarded the Knight's Cross for his work with the boat.

On its first two patrols no successes were reported. The boat left Kiel on 18 October on its first patrol, and joined its new base at La Pallice on 26 November. A month later it carried out another four week patrol that took it into 1942. For its third patrol *U-571* was given a change from the North Atlantic and this time was sent to the American eastern seaboard; here things were to be different.

U-271 under attack

During the evening of 29 March *U-571* opened its account, sinking the British steamer *Hertford* of 11,000 tons. Ten days later the Norwegian motor tanker *Koll* of 10,000 tons was hit by a torpedo and finished off by gunfire in the early evening of 8 April. Six days later the small American steamer *Margaret*, bound from Puerto Rico to Baltimore, was torpedoed and sunk. With three ships sunk, totalling nearly 25,000 tons, the crew of *U-571* were in a happier mood when they returned to La Pallice on 7 May.

Exactly five weeks later the U-boat set off for the Gulf of Mexico. The high expectations were realised in the morning of 7 July when an 8,000 ton British steamer *Umtata* was torpedoed and sunk. Twenty-one hours later an American steamer, the *J A Moffert Jr*, proved much more resilient. Although hit by two torpedoes and pounded with twenty 88mm shells the steamer of nearly 10,000 tons remained afloat and was later towed into harbour. The next day the gunners were in action again, sinking a small steamer registered in Honduras. Torpedoes were used again on 15 July in an early morning attack on an American ship *Pennsylvania Sun*. However, the 11,394 ton motor tanker was only damaged and remained afloat. This fourth patrol ended with *U-571* arriving back at base on 7 August.

After two months in port *U-571* was sent back to the North Atlantic and as on the previous two patrols in this area the boat returned, five weeks later, with no successes to report.

It was three days before Christmas when *U-571* set out to a new patrol area, south-west of the Azores, for its sixth cruise. The target for the pack that *U-571* joined was the supply line that was replenishing the American troops landed in North Africa for Operation Torch two months earlier. On 3 January Kapitänleutnant Hans-Jürgen Auffermann, returning from the Caribbean in *U-514*, sighted and attacked a tanker. The tanker was one of nine in convoy accompanied by HMS *Havelock* and three corvettes. Of the escort, two had faulty radar sets! On learning of the tankers, U-boat headquarters quickly ordered *U-571* and eleven other U-boats to the position. Five days later the pack intercepted the weakly escorted convoy and *U-436*, *U-124*, *U-522*, *U-575*, *U-442* and *U-441* all registered successes as seven of the nine tankers failed to arrive at their destination. Other U-boats, including *U-134*,

U-620 and *U-511* were not so fortunate with their attacks. Möhlmann fired at *Cliona* and thought he had hit the 9,000 ton Norwegian tanker, but what was thought to be torpedo detonations were in fact depth charge explosions fired from the overworked escort destroyer.

Along with other boats *U-571* refuelled from a milch-cow and it also took on a GSR aerial from *U-176*. The aerial had four separate sections arranged in a square round the foremast and gave a wide waveband cover with slight directional properties to its Rohide and Schwarz equipment. The new equipment was not to lead to any success on the patrol which ended at La Pallice on 19 February.

The U-boat spent most of March in port at a time when the Atlantic U-boats were causing havoc on the Atlantic convoy routes. It was not until the 25th that it commenced its seventh patrol, to the North Atlantic. In the early morning of 11 April attacks were made on convoys ON176 and ONS2 by *U-188*, *U-84* and *U-571*. The latter's contribution was the torpedoing of *Ingerfire*, a 4,000 ton Norwegian ship. Five ships were attacked by *U-571* with a three torpedo spread and a stern shot. *Ingerfire* broke in two and another was listing. Two detonations were heard by the U-boat. No further successes were reported and *U-571* arrived back at its French base on 1 May. Fortunately for the crew their boat remained in port all of May, while many of their comrades perished in that month, the most successful of the war against the U-boats. At the end of May Admiral Dönitz had withdrawn most of the Atlantic U-boats. The recall did not worry the commander of *U-571* as his boat was fitting out to patrol a new area, off West Africa.

On 3 June Kapitänleutnant Möhlmann conned *U-571* out of La Pallice for the last time. It was his eighth and last patrol with the boat, he had been in command for over two years.

Other U-boats had chalked up some successes off West Africa, mainly against independently routed ships during April and May, but *U-571* was not to be as fortunate. In fact, the U-boat was attacked and damaged by an aircraft of the SAAF No 26 Squadron on 22 July and immediately made tracks for base, arriving back on 1 September.

The U-boat was in port for over four months before being sent to sea again. It was now 1944 and Oberleutnant Gustav Lüssow had been appointed in command, succeeding Helmut Möhlmann. The U-boat was to join with others off the west coast of Ireland. On 18 January the new captain reported in to headquarters that he had attacked a destroyer with a T5 but that only an end-of-run explosion had been heard, after twelve minutes. This was the last message from the U-boat.

As with *U-271* earlier, *U-571* was under orders to reach an outward bound convoy as quickly as possible. Carrying out instructions the U-boat commander was ploughing through the heavy seas west of Galway when his boat was observed by the gunner of a Sunderland the same day, 28 January.

The flying boat, D-Dog of 461 Squadron, piloted by Australian Flight Lieutenant R. D. Lucas, was on an anti-U-boat sweep from its base at Pembroke Dock. When 180 miles west of Shannon *U-571* was sighted quite near the big convoy that was its target. The U-boat was steering a northerly course and its wake was first sighted by the front gunner, using binoculars, three miles away on the starboard bow. As the flying boat closed a white painted emblem was observed on the side of the conning tower. As the pilot ran in *U-571* made no effort to dive. When the Sunderland had closed to 3,000 yards the U-boat's guns opened fire. The front gunner of the flying boat held his fire until the range had closed to 1,000 yards, as the Sunderland carried out undulating evasive action through the, continual stream of flak. Tracer was also seen and a box barrage was put up but it followed the flying boat, always arriving just too late to register a hit.

When a quarter-of-a-mile dead astern of *U-571* the pilot executed a sharp turn to port and by the time it had halved the distance, the guns of the U-boat were silent and Flight Lieutenant Lucas was able to attack from the U-boat's port quarter without opposition. The first stick of four depth charges undershot, although the nearest entered the water only thirty yards from the conning tower. As the Sunderland flew over the target its crew counted ten bodies strewn about the conning tower and bandstand although the U-boat appeared undamaged. There was no sign of life on deck as the flying boat came in again, attacking from *U-571*'s starboard beam. A perfect straddle was achieved by the remaining two depth charges exploding each side of the conning tower.

One minute later an explosion was seen and the U-boat disintegrated. At the time the Sunderland was circling preparatory to taking photographs. A large patch of oil immediately appeared and wreckage and bodies were seen. There were some survivors and the flying boat released a dinghy but this unfortunately failed to inflate.

As soon as the news of the sinking was reported HMS *Vanquisher*, fifty miles to the eastward, was detached from the escort to search for survivors. The destroyer remained until darkness when it was ordered by the Commander-in-Chief Western Approaches to rejoin convoy SC151 and the B6 escort group.

As so often had happened, an old U-boat did not survive its first patrol under a new commander and the whole crew were lost.

There were no photographs taken of the attack because the evasive action of the flying boat was so violent that the rear-facing camera was wrenched from its mounting and its operator, the navigator, was thrown from the galley to the wardroom, where he was temporarily knocked unconscious. The Australian pilot was awarded the Distinguished Flying Cross for the sinking.

Operations against the convoy were suspended by Admiral Dönitz the following morning for a very strange reason. A Luftwaffe pilot had reported two to three hundred landing craft about 120 miles west of the Gironde estuary. Although an Allied invasion seemed improbable the Kriegsmarine were taking no chances following the attack on St Nazaire two years earlier. Boats outward-bound from Biscay bases were sent at high speed to intercept, and at 0800 one of these boats, *U-302*, reported sighting an air-escorted convoy steering a north-westerly course near the position reported by the aircraft. It appeared, therefore, that the aircraft's report was correct and that an invasion was indeed intended, although this was most unlikely in the absence of air attacks on western France and as the landing formation had appeared in the early afternoon. At 0830 all boats in the North Atlantic were ordered at full speed to the Biscay coast, but two hours later *U-302* reported that the ships which it had taken for a convoy had turned out to be Spanish trawlers, whereupon the boats were instructed to submerge and reoccupy their previous attack areas. This included those that had been searching for the outward-bound convoy.

This episode must have afforded the cryptoanalysts, and the Admiralty, much amusement at the time. Obviously, so as not to alert the Germans that they were reading their signals it certainly was not then made common knowledge in England.

The day after the invasion scare Allied aircraft were over the Bay of Biscay. They were returning to previously profitable areas from where they had been diverted by the actions of the U-boats to the west of Ireland and the stationing of 19 Group to Irish bases. The new patrols were routed further inshore to try to catch the U-boats using the swept channels cleared for the entering and leaving of their French bases. Only one U-boat had been sunk in the Bay in January.

Flight Sergeant L. D. Richards of No 172 Squadron, with his all NCO crew, had taken off from Chivenor in their Leigh light Wellington XIV MP813 K-King in darkness, at 2011, on 30 January for an anti-U-boat patrol over the Bay of Biscay. Nothing more was ever heard of them. The weather had closed in at Chivenor and at dawn a signal: 'Land at St Eval on completion of sortie', was sent. But by this time the crew had been dead for some hours.

What had happened was that soon after midnight the Wellington had picked up *U-364* completing its first patrol, returning to a French base. The Type VIIC U-boat had been launched from Flensburger Schiffsbau a year earlier and Oberleutnant Paul-Heinrich Sass had taken it on its first war patrol, from Kiel on 23 November, to the North Atlantic. Now, with no successes to report it was making for the French Atlantic coast when it was located.

The Wellington pilot switched on his Leigh light and attacked; depth charges were dropped, but at the same time the U-boat's gunners were on target and shot down the Wellington. The depth charges exploded and *U-364* was lost with all its crew.

The events were watched with some amazement by the crew of a Czech Liberator of 304 Squadron, patrolling west of Bordeaux. They told their story when they arrived back at Predannack. The pilot, Flight Sergeant S. Czeckalski, said that at 0027 they had picked up a blip, 20 degrees to starboard, at two miles. Turning on course the crew saw the Leigh light of another aircraft switched on, then the explosions of depth charges. After a steep turn the contact disappeared but a marine marker, was seen to be dropped.

Not for the first time in the U-boat war both the hunter and the hunted had been lost with the lives of all concerned.

CHAPTER THIRTEEN

Arctic Action

The Atlantic wolf packs had been broken up, but those in the Arctic were to last longer. The short operational career of *U-314* was spent entirely in that Northern theatre. The Type VIIC boat was launched from the Flenderwerft at Lübeck in mid-April 1943. Its commander, Kapitänleutnant Georg-Wilhelm Basse, was entitled to have an Olympic rings logo on the conning tower as he was one of the class of 1936, the year that the games were held in Berlin.

After the necessary exercises and training in the Baltic, *U-314* put out from Kiel, for the Atlantic, and refuelled at Kristiansand. Orders were then changed in the light of circumstances and when in the Norwegian port, on the 18th, the captain was told to proceed to northern waters and *U-314* was placed under the command of Captain U-boats, Norway. Three days later the boat put into Trondheim for a brief stay, where the periscope was repaired and a few adjustments for the new area of operations were carried out.

Leaving Trondheim, *U-314* joined a pack of U-boats and on completion of this mission was ordered to put in to Hammerfest. The U-boat took up its position in the pack on Christmas Eve and operated on an eastbound convoy. No contact was made as the shadower could not maintain contact. On Boxing Day *U-314* broke off operations to search for *Scharnhorst* survivors from the Battle of the North Cape. Next the U-boat took up position in various patrol lines, reconnaissance lines and attack areas near the Bear Island passage, and put into Hammerfest on 14 January. There was nothing Kapitänleutnant Basse could report from the seven locations he had been in on the patrol, except for the sighting of one aircraft and one drifting mine.

With the sinking of *Scharnhorst* the German fleet was left with no effective heavy ship in Northern Norway and so U-boats constituted the main threat against the Russian convoys. The northern based U-boats had only lost one of their number to the enemy during the whole of 1943, but now with the battleship menace removed the convoys could be better escorted by light forces.

As in many other theatres of operations January 1944 produced atrocious weather. In the Arctic a series of storms occurred which even for this area were unusually ferocious.

The first convoy of the year to sail, from Loch Ewe, commenced its voyage on 12 January and was unlucky from the start. A heavy gale off the Faroes forced five of the twenty ships to put back and the remainder were considerably delayed. The remaining ships, many of which were damaged, were forced to seek shelter in Iceland where they were reported by German agents. When the convoy proceeded on the 21st it was escorted by three cruisers, *Kent, Berwick* and *Bermuda*, with nine destroyers and two corvettes.

Through being forewarned, the Germans were waiting for the convoy. The Captain of U-boats Norway, Peters, considered that the constant occupation of the Bear Island passage by six boats was the maximum which could be achieved in order to ensure that there would be an adequate number of U-boats in readiness at Hammerfest, in case of the appearance of convoys. He also said:

> As the Bear Island passage presents unavoidable geographical restrictions to the enemy which do not permit him to exploit the superiority of his radar equipment in order to evade our U-boat positions, but more or less force him to pass right through them, it is to be expected that very strong anti-U-boat groups will continue to be used in the future. It is regrettable that owing to the lack of surface forces and aircraft we are unable to deal with these groups so near to our coasts.
>
> It is therefore up to the U-boats to fight their way through to the convoy and this will mean an increased use of T5 torpedoes.

The position on 25 January was that a group at sea sweeping a depth of twenty-five miles consisted of *U-739, U-278, U-360, U-425, U-965* and *U-601*. Proceeding from Jan Mayen to relieve *U-360* was

HMS *Meteor*

Convoy and Escort for Russia assemble at Iceland

U-737. There were two boats at Hammerfest, one in Narvik, four in Trondheim, three in Bergen, two at Kristiansand and one at Königsberg. Five U-boats were also on passage to or from the operational area.

Kapitänleutnant Basse in *U-314* and Oberleutnant Hans Dunkelberg in *U-716*, the boats at Hammerfest, put out together at 1300. In the evening *U-360* torpedoed and damaged the escort destroyer HMS *Obdurate*. Later *U-278* fired a spread of three FAT and sank an American steamer. Just after midnight *U-360* torpedoed and damaged one of the convoy and at much the same time *U-716*, which had quickly reached the Bear Island passage, also fired a spread of three FAT and sank an American steamer. The ship that *U-360* had damaged was later sunk by *U-957*. All three ships sunk were in the 7–8,000 ton category.

During the early hours *U-314* fired two T5's at a destroyer but they missed. The message from *U-314* timed 0250 gave its position and said:

Two T5 torpedoes on destroyer, one explosion heard after three-and-a-half minutes. Escort three destroyers ahead and four destroyers ahead to starboardd. Several steamers in column formation.

Following their successes the U-boats were transferred to the west where the next convoy, JW56B, which left Loch Ewe on the 22nd, had been reported by the Luftwaffe. The convoy had been delayed due to the scattering and weather damage to the previous convoy.

The sixteen ship convoy had fourteen U-boats ranged against it by the 29th as it entered the danger zone, two of them had been seen on the morning of the 30th.

U-313, U-314, U-472, U-601, U-636, U-716, U-737, U-739, U-956, U-278, U-425, U-957, U-965 and *U-990* were on the convoy and *U-312*, acting as the weather boat, was nearby. In the early hours, while searching for a U-boat at twenty knots, the destroyer leader, HMS *Hardy*, was torpedoed and had to be sunk by HMS *Venus*. The Norwegian destroyer *Stord* and HMS *Milne* were near missed. During the day *U-313, U-965* and *U-425* all made unsuccessful attacks on the convoy but in the evening two destroyers of the convoy escort struck back.

The two destroyers, HMS *Meteor* and HMS *Whitehall*, were an odd assortment. HMS *Meteor* had been launched just over two years earlier but the other was a veteran V and W class boat dating back to 1919. *Whitehall* had started the war with the 15th Destroyer Flotilla at Rosyth but spent from May-August 1942 in Sheerness Dockyard being converted to a long range escort. The previous October it had been part of the escort in the occupation of the Azores and at the end of the month had helped to sink *U-306* in the Atlantic. The crew were putting in plenty of sea time for now, three months later, they were in the Barents Sea.

The destroyers were on the starboard bow of the convoy at 1917, 180 miles north of the North Cape, when *Meteor* reported torpedoes approaching and almost immediately picked up an asdic contact. Twenty minutes later *Whitehall* joined. Depth charge attacks were carried out, then *Whitehall* reported she had lost touch. *Meteor* reported she was still in touch and continued attacking. At 2000 *Whitehall* picked up a radar contact three miles to the southward of her and immediately informed *Meteor* that torpedoes had been fired. The captain of *U-314* was making a last desperate effort to shake off his pursuers by a dash on the surface. A sweep by the destroyers was then commenced at seven knots. Forty-five minutes later *Whitehall* informed *Meteor* she was in contact with a U-boat on the port side, range just under a mile. The hunt, and attacks, continued until shortly before midnight. The five-hour hunt was reported as the most intense and interesting of the passage and was reported by the destroyers as 'inconclusive'. However, *U-314* was sunk during this time after spending just six weeks as a front boat. Neither it, nor any others in the pack, sank any of the convoy, which safely arrived at Kola Inlet on 1 February.

The Germans reported twelve T5 torpedoes fired, resulting in four destroyers sunk, three other hits and one possible hit and one premature explosion and three misses. A sinking of six destroyers was possible and perhaps even seven. Unfortunately for the Germans these claims were wildly out; only *Hardy* was sunk and *Obdurate* damaged.

The day before *U-314* was sunk Heinrich Schweich, in a

broadcast to the German people on U-boat attacks, talking of the Arctic said:

> In the Northern Arctic the Anglo-Americans have been forced to take very thorough precautions to be able to carry to Murmansk the military supplies so insistently demanded by the Soviets. They have used not only light, naval forces on this route, but also cruisers, battleships and aircraft carriers. The convoy with which our U-boats made contact a few days ago was not protected by such heavy units. The enemy believed he could make do with a strong destroyer screen and rely on favourable weather. However, this destroyer screen was extremely strong and when the first boat sighted the Murmansk-bound convoy, it became clear that every merchant ship was protected by two escort vessels. The core of the convoy was surrounded by a double protecting belt. Our commanders had first to deal with this escort force and this could only be done after the most violent engagements with the superior fire-power of the escort vessels.
>
> The first reports of enemy vessels sunk naturally dealt with destroyers. Later in the operations it became clear that, once again, the surprise blow had succeeded, with the result that all U-boats operating in the Far North were able to join in sinking valuable merchant tonnage.
>
> Tanks, cars, aircraft and other military equipment went down into the Arctic before they could be used against our troops on the Eastern Front.
>
> The operations took place on the shipping route between the Arctic and the Barents Sea, north of Murmansk. In addition to the enemy sea escort, the attackers had to overcome almost incredible weather conditions. For hours on end, German lookouts had to contend with visibility of 500 metres or less in which their boat was liable to collide with another U-boat or with an enemy escort vessel. In view of these conditions, our U-boats' success in the Arctic is all the more remarkable.

January drew to a close with fourteen boats already sunk. Two-and-a-half months earlier wolf packs, grouped in three lines had attempted to stop homeward bound convoys from reaching the

United Kingdom without any notable success, now they were operating singly. The reading of enemy signals had allowed the convoys to be diverted and instead of finding merchantment waiting to be picked off the U-boats found they were being detected by increasingly large numbers of escort and hunter groups. There was no respite at night as the ASV radar picked them up and they were attacked by Leigh light aircraft.

The German submariners fought bravely but as Admiral Dönitz eventually realised the odds were stacked too heavily against them in their existing boats.

The Arctic U-boats continued to hunt the Russian convoys in packs and indeed the last centrally directed wolf pack operation in the Atlantic took place, with heavy losses, in mid-February, but by the end of January it is fair to say that the Allies had achieved enough to ensure the *Defeat of the Wolf Packs*.

Glossary

ASV	Air to Surface Vessel (radar)
B.Dienst	German observation service (Beobachtungs-Dienst)
CAM	Catapult Aircraft Merchantman
Chance light	Mobile light that illuminates the end of a runway and can only be seen from the ground
D/F	Direction Finder
Enigma	German coding machine
ERA	Engine Room Artificer
FAT	FederApparatTorpedo – a torpedo with a pre-set course
GSR	German Search Receiver
H_2S	Radar aid to navigation and target identification
H/F	High Frequency
HMCS	His Majesty's Canadian Ship
MAC	Merchant Aircraft Carrier
MGB	Motor Gun Boat
ML	Motor Launch
MTB	Motor Torpedo Boat
NCO	Non-Commissioned Officer
PDC	Personnel Dispersal Centre
RP	Rocket Projectile
R/T	Radio Telephony
Rudelsystem	Wolf Pack
SBT	Submarine Bubble Target
SAAF	South African Air Force
Sandra Light	Searchlight(s) used to guide aircraft to their base
SOE	Senior Officer of Escorts

SOS	Save Our Souls – International distress call
TS	Training Station
USAAF	United States Army Air Force
USN	United States Navy
VLR	Very Long Range
W/T	Wireless Telegraphy

Index

215